The History of the UFC Book 1

James Bren

Published by James Bren, 2025.

THE HISTORY OF THE UFC BOOK 1

First edition. July 6, 2025.

ISBN: 979-8230558569

Written by James Bren.

THE HISTORY OF THE UFC

BOOK 1

Forging a Fighting Empire: Unraveling the Epic Journey of the UFC

James Bren

Disclaimer

This book, "History of the UFC," authored by James Bren, is a comprehensive exploration of the UFC's fascinating journey. The content within is based on publicly available information up to my last knowledge update in January 2022.

While every effort has been made to ensure accuracy, the dynamic nature of the UFC's history may result in occasional inaccuracies or omissions. Additionally, the opinions expressed in this book are those of the author and not necessarily reflective of the UFC's official stance.

Readers are encouraged to cross-reference information with up-to-date sources and official UFC channels for the latest developments. This book is not an official UFC publication, but rather an independent effort to present the sport's history in an engaging manner.

Published by James Bren

Chapters

Introduction: Inception and Evolution of the Ultimate Fighting Championship

In the vast arena of combat sports, where warriors from different disciplines strive to prove their supremacy, one organization has risen to unparalleled prominence—the Ultimate Fighting Championship (UFC). From its humble beginnings to becoming a global juggernaut, the UFC's journey is a tale of ambition, innovation, and unwavering determination.

The roots of the UFC can be traced back to the early 1990s, a time when the world of martial arts was filled with passionate debates about which fighting style reigned supreme. Amidst these discussions, a radical idea took shape in the minds of businessman Art Davie and Brazilian Jiu-Jitsu expert Rorion Gracie. They sought to create an event that would bring together fighters from various disciplines to compete against each other with minimal rules—a concept that would later be known as no holds barred.

On November 12, 1993, this audacious vision materialized in Denver, Colorado, as the inaugural UFC event unfolded. With a makeshift Octagon as their battleground, fighters from diverse backgrounds—karate, boxing, sumo wrestling, Brazilian Jiu-Jitsu, and more—stepped into the spotlight, ready to prove the effectiveness of their art. Little did they know that they were about to pave the way for a revolutionary sport that would captivate the world.

The early UFC events were met with both intrigue and skepticism. Critics decried the perceived brutality and lack of regulations, while supporters hailed it as the ultimate test of martial arts skill. The novelty of seeing different combat styles clash, often with unpredictable results, drew attention and curiosity from fans and detractors alike.

As the UFC gained popularity, it also faced significant challenges. Several states in the United States banned the events, and authorities questioned its legality and safety. This forced the UFC to introspect and adapt. In response, they embraced the need for greater structure and safety measures, leading to the formulation of the Unified Rules of Mixed Martial Arts.

Despite the initial controversies, the UFC refused to be deterred. Under new ownership led by brothers Lorenzo and Frank Fertitta, along with the business acumen of Dana White, the promotion underwent a transformation that would forever change the landscape of combat sports. Their passion and commitment breathed new life into the UFC, guiding it towards becoming a professional and mainstream organization.

With rigorous regulations, weight classes, and a focus on athlete safety, the UFC emerged as a legitimate sport that demanded respect. It drew in new talent from across the globe and witnessed the rise of legendary fighters, each bringing their unique flair and skill to the Octagon. The fusion of multiple martial arts disciplines gave birth to a dynamic and electrifying new style—the art of mixed martial arts.

As the UFC solidified its reputation, it began to expand its reach far beyond American borders. International events in Brazil, Japan, the United Kingdom, and various other countries introduced the UFC to a diverse global audience. Televised broadcasts and pay-per-view events propelled the organization into households worldwide, making household names of fighters and captivating fans from all walks of life.

The UFC's ascent was accompanied by incredible achievements, record-breaking pay-per-view buys, and monumental fight nights that etched themselves into sports history. The Octagon became a proving ground for courage, skill, and resilience, where fighters faced adversity head-on and emerged as true champions.

The inception and evolution of the Ultimate Fighting Championship are a testament to the indomitable spirit of its creators and the fighters who embraced its challenges. From its controversial beginnings to its journey towards global dominance, the UFC's story is one of perseverance, innovation, and passion. It is a saga that has forever altered the world of combat sports and left an indelible mark on the hearts of millions of fans worldwide. As we delve deeper into the annals of UFC history, we will witness the triumphs, setbacks, and unforgettable moments that have shaped this extraordinary organization into what it is today—the epitome of strength, skill, and sheer determination in the world of mixed martial arts.

Chapter 1

Early 1990s Competition – The Birth of the Ultimate Fighting Championship

In the early 1990s, the world of martial arts and combat sports was a dynamic and diverse landscape, with practitioners of different disciplines passionately advocating for the supremacy of their respective arts. It was in the midst of this fervent environment that an audacious and groundbreaking idea took shape—the creation of the Ultimate Fighting Championship (UFC). Driven by the desire to determine the most effective martial art in real combat scenarios, the UFC would emerge as a platform that would forever revolutionize the world of combat sports.

The seeds of the UFC were planted in the minds of two visionary men, Art Davie and Rorion Gracie. Together, they embarked on a mission to bring to life an eight-man single-elimination tournament, aptly named "War of the Worlds." This bold and ambitious endeavor sought to pit fighters from various martial arts disciplines against one another, with minimal rules, in a quest to identify the ultimate fighting technique.

The inspiration for "War of the Worlds" came from the "Gracies in Action" video series, which showcased Gracie Jiu-Jitsu students effortlessly defeating practitioners of different martial arts in Vale Tudo matches—a form of Brazilian no-holds-barred combat. Rorion Gracie, a master of Brazilian Jiu-Jitsu and a member of the esteemed Gracie family, eagerly embraced the opportunity to showcase and promote his family's revered martial art on a grand stage.

To turn their visionary concept into reality, Art Davie approached renowned filmmaker and screenwriter John Milius to be part of the venture. Milius, known for his work on iconic movies such as "Apocalypse Now" and "Conan the Barbarian," eagerly embraced the opportunity to contribute his creative expertise to the project. With the support of 28 investors, WOW Promotions was established to develop the tournament into a television franchise.

The idea behind "War of the Worlds" was to present a real-life fighting tournament akin to popular video games like Street Fighter and Mortal Kombat. Fighters hailing from diverse disciplines would enter the Octagon to face off against opponents from different styles, with the aim of finding the ultimate martial art—the art that could prevail in any combat situation.

One of the most iconic aspects of the UFC is its distinct fighting arena—the Octagon. To visually differentiate the UFC from traditional boxing and wrestling events, the organizers tasked Jason Cusson, a talented video and film art director, with designing an innovative and visually captivating setting for the tournament.

Traditional roped rings were quickly dismissed due to concerns about fighter safety and potential escapes during grappling exchanges. After exploring several creative ideas, Cusson arrived at a groundbreaking concept—the Octagon. An eight-sided enclosure surrounded by chain-link fence, the Octagon became the signature setting for UFC events, symbolizing the electrifying and unbounded nature of the competition.

With the vision of WOW Promotions taking shape, the event was officially rebranded as "The Ultimate Fighting Championship" in May 1993. The organization found a partnership with Semaphore Entertainment Group (SEG), a pioneering company in pay-per-view television, which enabled the UFC to reach a global audience.

On November 12, 1993, the inaugural UFC event, UFC 1, made its much-anticipated debut at the McNichols Sports Arena in Denver, Colorado. The tournament featured an intriguing lineup of fighters hailing from diverse martial arts backgrounds. Among the competitors were Kevin Rosier, a formidable kickboxer; Patrick Smith, a skilled taekwondo practitioner; Gerard Gordeau, a savate fighter; Zane Frazier, an expert in karate; Ken Shamrock, a skilled shootfighter; Teila

Tuli, a towering sumo wrestler; Art Jimmerson, a professional boxer; and the young Brazilian Jiu-Jitsu black belt Royce Gracie, who was chosen to represent the Gracie family.

UFC 1 marked a captivating display of different styles clashing inside the Octagon. Fighters, each with their unique skill sets, faced off against opponents with vastly different backgrounds, leading to intriguing matchups and unpredictable outcomes.

As the night progressed, it became evident that Royce Gracie's submission prowess was unparalleled. Utilizing his Brazilian Jiu-Jitsu expertise, Gracie masterfully defeated his opponents one by one, showcasing the effectiveness of Gracie Jiu-Jitsu in real combat scenarios.

Royce Gracie's victories in UFC 1 highlighted the significance of grappling and submission techniques, which were often overlooked or underestimated in traditional martial arts competitions. His triumphs not only solidified his status as a skilled martial artist but also brought international recognition to Brazilian Jiu-Jitsu, elevating it to the forefront of the martial arts world.

The Success of UFC 1 and Beyond

The resounding success of UFC 1 surpassed all expectations, captivating the imagination of sports enthusiasts and martial arts aficionados worldwide. The event garnered an impressive 86,592 pay-per-view television subscribers, proving that there was a genuine appetite for unfiltered and raw combat sports.

Despite initial skepticism and concerns surrounding the no-holds-barred nature of the competition, the UFC remained steadfast in its mission. Subsequent events continued to push boundaries and captivate audiences, establishing the UFC as a pioneering platform for martial artists to test their skills and styles on a global stage.

Contrary to popular belief, the promoters behind the UFC never viewed it as a one-night spectacle. Instead, they envisioned the UFC as an ongoing series of fighting tournaments—a franchise with a future beyond its inaugural night. Campbell McLaren, one of the executives at SEG, even offered WOW Promotions a five-year joint development deal, underlining the belief in the UFC as a sustainable and enduring venture.

As the early 1990s drew to a close, the UFC had firmly established itself as a force to be reckoned with in the world of combat sports. Its evolution from a one-night spectacle to an ongoing series of events marked the beginning of an extraordinary journey that would elevate the UFC to a global phenomenon.

The early 1990s competition in the UFC showcased a diverse array of fighters, styles, and skills. Alongside Royce Gracie, iconic names such as Ken Shamrock, Patrick Smith, Dan Severn, Marco Ruas, Gary Goodridge, Don Frye, and others graced the Octagon, leaving an indelible mark on the history of mixed martial arts.

The UFC's commitment to innovation and adaptation would become hallmarks of the organization's journey, and its impact on the world of combat sports would resonate for generations to come. As the chapters unfold, we will explore the pivotal moments, legendary fighters, and historic events that shaped the UFC's transformation into a global powerhouse and a beacon of strength and intensity in the world of martial arts. Welcome to the captivating world of the Ultimate Fighting Championship.

Enhance your understanding of the UFC's rich tapestry with "UFC: A Visual History" by Thomas Gerbasi. This visual feast is a perfect companion to the chapter you've just explored. Immerse yourself in the raw intensity and gripping narratives that shaped the UFC's incredible journey. Gerbasi's keen insights and vivid visuals provide a ringside seat to the heart-pounding evolution of the sport. A must-read for those hungry for more behind-the-scenes stories and iconic moments. Grab your copy and extend your exploration of the UFC's thrilling history!

Chapter 2

Tightening up of the Rules - Evolving Towards Legitimacy

As the Ultimate Fighting Championship (UFC) surged into the mid-1990s, its early tagline of "There are no rules" proved to be a provocative statement that captured the attention of fight fans and critics alike. In truth, even in its infancy, the UFC operated with limited rules, but compared to other established combat sports, its ruleset was indeed minimalist, allowing for a wide range of techniques and strategies to be employed in the fights. As the organization grappled with its reputation as an extremely violent spectacle, significant changes were on the horizon. The tightening up of the rules would become a pivotal turning point for the UFC, guiding it towards legitimacy and acceptance in the world of combat sports.

The early years of the UFC were marked by an experimental atmosphere, where the concept of "no rules" served as a provocative marketing tactic. In reality, the UFC did have a set of guidelines to ensure the safety and fairness of the fighters. However, compared to the more established sports of the time, the UFC allowed for a broader spectrum of techniques and approaches to be utilized, including strikes, grappling, and submissions.

At the heart of the early UFC events was the desire to determine the most effective martial art in a real combat setting. This led to a diverse roster of competitors, each representing various martial arts disciplines, from Brazilian Jiu-Jitsu to boxing to wrestling.

As fighters with vastly different skillsets clashed inside the Octagon, fans were treated to a fascinating display of mixed martial arts, with each event showcasing a unique blend of techniques and strategies.

In some instances, competitors made informal agreements before their matches, like Jason Fairn and Guy Mezger, who decided not to pull each other's hair during their UFC 4 qualifying match, as they both sported ponytails. These moments highlighted the pioneering nature of the early UFC events and the willingness of the fighters to adapt to the evolving landscape.

As the UFC continued to grow in popularity, UFC 5 introduced a momentous change with the introduction of the first singles match, known as "The Superfight." This particular bout featured a highly anticipated rematch between three-time champion Royce Gracie and Ken Shamrock. Originally designed as a non-tournament match to determine the first reigning UFC Champion, "The Superfight" would eventually transform the landscape of UFC competitions.

"The Superfight" concept provided an opportunity for high-profile matchups that extended beyond the traditional one-night tournament format. It allowed for marquee fighters to face each other in a longer and more intense setting, enticing fans with the promise of epic showdowns between legendary competitors.

As the popularity of "The Superfight" grew, it led to a shift in focus away from the traditional tournament-style matches. The UFC gradually phased out the tournament format, and the "Superfight" became a prominent fixture in future events. The decision to prioritize longer, more intense singles matches was aimed at allowing fighters to showcase their skills and techniques in greater depth, promoting rivalries and building narratives around key matchups.

While the introduction of "The Superfight" brought new excitement to the UFC, it was not without its challenges. The first "Superfight" at UFC 5, featuring Royce Gracie and Ken Shamrock, proved to be a double-edged sword. Although highly anticipated, the bout did not deliver the anticipated excitement.

Within the first minute of the fight, Shamrock managed to knock Gracie to the ground, and for the next 30 minutes, the fighters found themselves in a grappling stalemate with little action. The lack of significant progress or action frustrated the audience, and boos echoed throughout the arena.

The bout, originally scheduled for a 30-minute duration, exceeded its allotted time limit for the pay-per-view broadcast. Spectator protests led to an additional 5 minutes of extra time, but even that failed to break the stalemate. After a grueling 36 minutes, the fight was declared a draw, leaving fans and critics alike dissatisfied.

The Introduction of Time Limits, Judges, and Referees

The outcome of the controversial Gracie vs. Shamrock "Superfight" had a profound impact on the UFC's future direction. Determined to prevent similar anticlimactic outcomes in the future, the UFC implemented a series of rule changes.

One of the most significant changes was the introduction of time limits to all matches. This ensured that fights had a definitive end, avoiding the potential for inconclusive and monotonous contests. Time limits forced fighters to be more strategic and calculated in their approach, adding an element of urgency to each bout.

To avoid inconclusive draws like the Gracie vs. Shamrock fight, judges were brought in to score matches in the event of a draw. This allowed for a clear winner to be determined, further adding to the legitimacy of the UFC as a sport.

Furthermore, authorized referees were empowered to stand up fighters and restart the bout if they detected excessive inactivity or stalling. This proactive approach ensured that the action remained dynamic and exciting, discouraging fighters from employing overly defensive strategies that led to stalemate situations.

As the UFC continued to evolve, it sought to expand its reach beyond the borders of the continental United States. In 1996, UFC 8 marked the organization's first venture outside the mainland, with Bayamón, Puerto Rico, playing host to this historic event. This international foray demonstrated the UFC's growing popularity and global appeal.

The following year, in 1997, the UFC made its debut in Japan with "Ultimate Japan." This marked another milestone as the UFC held its first foreign event, solidifying its status as a truly international brand.

The tightening up of the rules in the UFC represented a pivotal turning point in its journey towards legitimacy and acceptance. Gone were the days of "no rules," as the organization adopted a more structured approach, striking a balance between safety and the display of martial arts skills.

As the UFC phased out the tournament format in favor of "Superfights" and implemented time limits, judges, and authorized referees, the organization sought to deliver more exciting and action-packed contests to its growing audience. The expansion beyond the continental United States showcased the UFC's ambition to become a global powerhouse in the world of combat sports.

In the chapters to come, we will delve deeper into the UFC's ongoing transformation, exploring the further evolution of its rules, the emergence of legendary fighters, and the iconic events that solidified its position as the premier organization in mixed martial arts.

Join us on this enthralling journey as we witness the UFC's relentless pursuit of greatness and its rise to the pinnacle of combat sports on the world stage.

Welcome to the captivating world of the Ultimate Fighting Championship.

Chapter 3

Late 1990s Controversy and Reform - The Path to Sanctioning and Legitimacy

As the Ultimate Fighting Championship (UFC) continued to gain momentum and popularity, its violent nature began to draw the attention of U.S. authorities, leading to a series of events that would shape the future of mixed martial arts (MMA) and the UFC itself. The late 1990s proved to be a tumultuous period for the organization as it faced mounting controversy, bans, and public scrutiny. However, it was also a time of crucial reform and evolution, as the UFC sought to work with state athletic commissions, modify its rules, and gain legitimacy as a regulated sport.

The rise of the UFC did not go unnoticed, and its no-holds-barred and unregulated nature quickly drew the ire of many, including U.S. Senator John McCain. In 1996, Senator McCain was shown a tape of the early UFC events and was immediately appalled by the brutal and violent nature of the sport. He took a stand against the UFC, publicly denouncing it as "human cockfighting" and calling for its ban. Senator McCain's vocal opposition to the UFC brought the sport into the national spotlight and raised significant concerns about its safety and legality.

Senator McCain's campaign against the UFC gained traction, leading to a domino effect of state bans on "no-holds-barred" fighting, a term often used to describe the unregulated and violent nature of early MMA competitions. Thirty-six states passed laws that banned or severely restricted such events, dealing a significant blow to the UFC's ability to host events across the United States. Notably, New York enacted its ban on the eve of UFC 12, forcing the event to relocate to Dothan, Alabama. These bans and restrictions threatened the very existence of the UFC and raised questions about the future of the sport.

In the face of mounting criticism and the threat of extinction, the UFC recognized the need for change. Determined to salvage the sport and gain legitimacy, the organization embarked on a path of cooperation with state athletic commissions and underwent significant reforms.

The UFC began to work closely with athletic commissions, seeking their input and guidance to modify the rules and ensure that the sport met acceptable safety standards. The goal was to retain the essence of striking and grappling while making the sport more palatable to regulators and the general public.

UFC 12, held in 1997, marked a significant turning point in the organization's history. It saw the introduction of weight classes, a move aimed at creating more balanced and competitive matchups. Weight classes provided fighters with a fairer playing field and reduced the risk of smaller competitors facing significantly larger opponents.

Subsequent UFC events continued to implement new regulations and safety measures. UFC 14 made the use of gloves mandatory, a crucial step to protect fighters' hands and reduce the risk of cuts and injuries. At the same time, strikes to the head of a downed opponent were banned, reflecting the organization's commitment to protecting fighters from unnecessary harm.

UFC 15 saw further rule changes, including limitations on hair pulling and the banning of strikes to the back of the neck and head, headbutting, small-joint manipulations, and groin strikes. These changes aimed to eliminate dangerous and potentially life-threatening techniques from the Octagon, ensuring a safer environment for all competitors.

With five-minute rounds introduced at UFC 21, the UFC took another step towards rebranding itself as a sport rather than a spectacle. The introduction of rounds added structure to the fights and allowed fighters to strategize and adapt throughout the contest. This format mirrored that of other established combat sports, further legitimizing the UFC in the eyes of regulators and fans.

To gain acceptance from state athletic commissions and regulators, the UFC, under the leadership of Jeff Blatnick, John McCarthy, and matchmaker Joe Silva, created a comprehensive manual of policies, procedures, codes of conduct, and rules. This manual served as a crucial tool in getting the UFC sanctioned by various athletic commissions across the United States. Many of the rules and protocols outlined in this manual continue to influence the sport to this day.

Jeff Blatnick and John McCarthy took it upon themselves to travel around the country, meeting with state athletic commissions, and actively addressing concerns about the sport's safety and legitimacy. Through their efforts, they sought to demonstrate that MMA was not a barbaric and inhumane endeavor but a legitimate athletic competition with rules and regulations in place to ensure fighter safety.

Their tireless work in educating regulators and changing perceptions had a profound impact, and by April 2000, their efforts had borne fruit. California was set to become the first state in the U.S. to sign off on a set of codified rules that governed MMA, setting a precedent for other states to follow suit.

As the UFC continued to work towards its goals, it faced challenges in securing home-video releases for its events. Despite these obstacles, the UFC sought opportunities to host events in smaller U.S. markets. Venues like the Lake Charles Civic Center and states like Iowa, Mississippi, Louisiana, Wyoming, and Alabama became hosts to UFC events. These events allowed the UFC to reach new audiences and build a following in regions less accustomed to hosting professional sporting events.

In 2000, the International Fighting Championships (IFC) achieved a significant milestone by securing the first U.S. sanctioned MMA event. This momentous occasion was a testament to the UFC's broader impact on the MMA landscape and served as motivation for the UFC to continue its efforts to gain acceptance and regulation.

Just two months after the IFC's groundbreaking event, the UFC held its first sanctioned competition, UFC 28. Under the jurisdiction of the New Jersey State Athletic Control Board's "Unified Rules," the UFC took another stride towards solidifying its status as a legitimate and regulated sport.

The late 1990s were a defining period for the UFC, marked by controversy, bans, and a struggle for legitimacy. However, it was also a time of crucial reform and evolution. Through cooperation with state athletic commissions, the implementation of safety measures, and the gradual transformation of its rules and regulations, the UFC sought to shed its image as a spectacle of violence and rebrand itself as a legitimate sport.

The tireless efforts of individuals like Jeff Blatnick and John McCarthy in educating regulators and changing perceptions played a vital role in the UFC's journey towards acceptance. The organization's willingness to evolve and cooperate with regulators demonstrated a commitment to safety and fairness in the sport.

As the UFC continued to work towards its goal of becoming a sanctioned and respected sport, it would face new challenges and opportunities. The journey towards legitimacy and acceptance was far from over, but the groundwork laid in the late 1990s paved the way for the UFC's rise to unprecedented heights in the world of combat sports.

Chapter 4

2001 and the Beginning of the Zuffa Era - A New Dawn for the UFC

The year 2001 marked a seismic shift in the history of the Ultimate Fighting Championship (UFC). After years of battling to secure sanctioning and struggling financially, the UFC found itself on the brink of bankruptcy. However, a fortuitous opportunity arose when Station Casinos executives Frank and Lorenzo Fertitta, along with their business partner Dana White, stepped in with an audacious offer to purchase the struggling organization. This pivotal moment would lead to the birth of the Zuffa era, heralding a new dawn for the UFC and changing the landscape of mixed martial arts forever.

The Acquisition of the UFC and the Birth of Zuffa

The early 2000s were a precarious time for the UFC. The organization had faced significant backlash and legal challenges due to its no-holds-barred and unregulated nature. In the midst of financial difficulties, Semaphore Entertainment Group (SEG), the parent company of the UFC, was eager to find a buyer. Frank and Lorenzo Fertitta, successful entrepreneurs and avid fight fans, recognized the untapped potential in the UFC. They saw an opportunity to breathe new life into the struggling promotion and reshape the future of combat sports.

In January 2001, the Fertittas, in collaboration with Dana White, made a bold move by acquiring the UFC for $2 million. The trio established Zuffa, LLC, as the parent entity that would control and revitalize the UFC. With this acquisition, a new chapter in the UFC's history began, and the trajectory of the sport would be forever altered.

Critics questioned the Fertittas' decision to invest in an organization that lacked tangible assets. However, Lorenzo Fertitta understood the true value of the UFC lay in its brand and the three iconic letters: UFC. Despite its controversies and challenges, the UFC had already left a lasting impression on both fight fans and the broader public. Lorenzo recognized that the UFC brand had become synonymous with a unique style of combat sports entertainment, evoking strong emotions and sparking conversations everywhere it was mentioned.

Zuffa's strategic vision extended beyond tangible assets; they aimed to leverage the UFC's brand recognition to breathe new life into the promotion and capture the imagination of sports enthusiasts worldwide. With the acquisition of the trademark, Zuffa not only gained control of the UFC's assets but also inherited the immense potential to transform the organization into a global sporting phenomenon.

In addition to the trademark, Zuffa acquired the iconic wooden octagon, the symbolic centerpiece of the UFC's combat arena. The octagon had become an instantly recognizable symbol of the UFC's unique approach to martial arts competition. This iconic structure, with its eight-sided design, would become synonymous with the UFC's distinctive brand identity.

Zuffa also inherited a roster of fighters, albeit a modest one, with around a dozen fighter contracts. These fighters represented the diverse talent pool that would be the backbone of the organization's revitalization efforts. Zuffa's goal was clear: to cultivate a roster of skilled athletes from various disciplines who could showcase their talents in the Octagon and captivate audiences around the world.

Zuffa's business acumen was evident as they actively pursued opportunities to expand the UFC's reach and secure media partnerships. They recognized the importance of home entertainment and struck a deal to purchase the UFC's DVD rights from Lionsgate for an additional two million dollars. This strategic move allowed the UFC's exciting events and memorable moments to be shared with fans beyond the confines of live broadcasts.

Moreover, Zuffa embarked on a mission to secure media partnerships that would amplify the UFC's visibility. The promotion's exciting and unpredictable fights, combined with Zuffa's dedication to promoting the UFC as a legitimate sport, made it an attractive proposition for television networks.

Through these partnerships, the UFC's reach extended to new audiences, helping to cultivate a growing fan base around the world.

One of the most significant aspects of the Zuffa era was its commitment to transforming the UFC from a spectacle of controversy to a legitimate sport. Zuffa understood that the key to the UFC's long-term success was striking a delicate balance between the raw excitement of the sport and the need for a more regulated and professional approach.

Zuffa began implementing safety measures and regulations aimed at ensuring the well-being of the fighters and promoting a fair and competitive environment. Among the key changes were the introduction of weight classes, mandatory gloves for all fighters, and the prohibition of dangerous techniques that posed unnecessary risks to fighters.

The implementation of weight classes was a game-changer, allowing for more equitable matchups and preventing fighters from facing opponents with significant size advantages. Mandatory gloves not only protected the fighters' hands but also helped minimize cuts and injuries during intense bouts.

Zuffa's commitment to safety and athlete welfare extended to the hiring of experienced referees and judges to oversee fights. This move ensured that the outcome of each bout was decided fairly and impartially.

Moreover, Zuffa's embrace of regulations and safety measures was an essential step towards gaining official sanctioning in various states and countries. As more athletic commissions recognized the UFC as a legitimate sport adhering to recognized rules, the promotion's reputation and acceptance continued to grow.

Under Zuffa's dynamic leadership, the UFC embarked on a journey of global expansion. The Fertittas and Dana White recognized the immense potential of the UFC as an international sporting spectacle. They sought to introduce the UFC to new territories and cultures, tapping into previously untapped markets around the world.

As part of its international expansion, Zuffa hosted events in various countries, bringing the excitement of the UFC to new audiences. The promotion's commitment to showcasing local talent from different regions further endeared it to fans worldwide.

The year 2001 marked the beginning of the Zuffa era, a period that would forever alter the course of the UFC and the sport of mixed martial arts. The strategic vision, business acumen, and commitment to the UFC brand exhibited by the Fertittas and Dana White laid the foundation for a new era of prosperity and excitement.

Zuffa's acquisition of the UFC transformed a struggling promotion into a global sporting phenomenon. Their strategic moves, embracing of regulations, expansion of media partnerships, and commitment to athlete safety catapulted the UFC to new heights of popularity and acceptance.

The Zuffa era would go on to produce some of the most iconic and memorable moments in MMA history. The UFC became a cultural sensation, capturing the hearts of fight fans worldwide and breaking barriers to achieve mainstream acceptance. As the UFC's influence continued to grow, the Zuffa era heralded a new era of prosperity and excitement, forever leaving its indelible mark on the world of combat sports.

The journey towards global dominance had only just begun, and the UFC's future looked brighter than ever before.

Chapter 5

Struggle for Survival and Turnaround - Triumph Over Adversity

The early 2000s marked a period of rejuvenation and transformation for the Ultimate Fighting Championship (UFC) under the leadership of Zuffa, LLC. However, despite the newfound success, the organization was still facing significant financial challenges. Nevertheless, Zuffa remained steadfast in its commitment to elevating mixed martial arts (MMA) and turning the UFC into a mainstream sport. This chapter delves into the struggles, pivotal events, and determined efforts that ultimately led to the UFC's triumphant turnaround and emergence as a global sporting phenomenon.

Following the Zuffa purchase, the UFC began a slow but steady ascent in popularity. This progress was fueled by a combination of factors, including enhanced advertising, increased corporate sponsorships, the return to cable pay-per-view, and the release of home video and DVD compilations of past events. As the organization found its footing under Zuffa's ownership, the UFC started gaining traction among both hardcore fight fans and a broader audience.

Corporate sponsorships played a crucial role in bolstering the UFC's financial stability. Brands like Harley-Davidson, Bud Light, and Toyo Tires aligned themselves with the UFC, recognizing the sport's growing appeal and potential as a powerful marketing platform. These sponsorships not only provided financial support but also lent credibility to the UFC as a legitimate sporting organization.

Zuffa's commitment to broadening the UFC's reach led to significant television deals that brought the sport to a larger audience. In June 2002, The Best Damn Sports Show Period aired the first-ever mixed martial arts match on American cable television, featuring Chuck Liddell vs. Vitor Belfort at UFC 37.5. This groundbreaking moment exposed the sport to a broader audience and generated considerable interest.

Furthermore, FSN continued to air highlight shows from the UFC, which helped build momentum and attract new fans. Television exposure played a crucial role in establishing the UFC as a legitimate and entertaining sport.

One pivotal factor in the UFC's turnaround was its ability to secure larger venues for events, leading to increased live gate revenue. Prominent casino venues like the Trump Taj Mahal and the MGM Grand Garden Arena hosted UFC events, drawing substantial crowds and generating revenue. The UFC's growing popularity allowed it to outgrow smaller arenas, and it was now setting its sights on bigger stages.

Another crucial element of the UFC's resurgence was its return to cable pay-per-view. By partnering with established pay-per-view providers, Zuffa ensured that fans across the country could access and enjoy the exhilarating UFC events from the comfort of their homes. The pay-per-view model provided a reliable revenue stream and allowed the UFC to showcase its exciting fight cards to a broader audience.

UFC 40, held at the MGM Grand Arena, proved to be a turning point for the UFC and a milestone event in the Zuffa era. With a near sellout crowd of 13,022 and an impressive 150,000 pay-per-view buys, UFC 40 demonstrated the UFC's potential for mainstream success.

The event was headlined by a highly anticipated championship match between Tito Ortiz, the reigning UFC Light Heavyweight Champion, and Ken Shamrock, a legendary figure in MMA and professional wrestling. The match not only reignited a long-standing rivalry but also captivated a wide audience, drawing attention from media outlets like ESPN and USA Today.

UFC 40's success came at a critical juncture when the UFC was struggling financially. Prior to this event, Zuffa's previous shows had garnered an average of a mere 45,000 pay-per-view buys per event, putting the organization on the brink of bankruptcy. The triumph of

UFC 40 offered a glimmer of hope and provided a crucial lifeline for the UFC's future.

One significant factor in UFC 40's success was the marketing power of crossover athletes, particularly those transitioning from professional wrestling to MMA and vice versa. This practice had its roots in Japan's Pride Fighting Championships and proved to be a potent tool in attracting new audiences to the UFC.

The anticipation and energy surrounding UFC 40 suggested that mixed martial arts had the potential to captivate a mainstream audience and become a major player in the sports industry.

UFC 40's impact was profound, both within the organization and among the MMA community at large. Long-time UFC referee John McCarthy, who had been an observer of the sport's evolution since its early days, shared his perspective on the pivotal event:

"When that show (UFC 40) happened, I honestly felt like it was going to make it. Throughout the years, things were happening, and everything always looked bleak. It always looked like, this is it, this is going to be the last time. This is going to be the last year. But, when I was standing in the Octagon at UFC 40, I remember standing there before the Ortiz/Shamrock fight and looking around. The energy of that fight, it was phenomenal, and it was the first time I honestly said, it's going to make it." – "Big" John McCarthy

Despite the success of UFC 40, Zuffa was still grappling with financial deficits. By 2004, the organization had accumulated losses amounting to $34 million since the initial purchase. However, this financial burden did not deter the Fertitta brothers and Dana White from their mission to elevate the UFC and solidify its position as a premier sporting brand.

Determined to overcome financial challenges, Zuffa continued to invest in the promotion, signing top talent and producing high-quality events. They believed in the UFC's potential and were committed to providing fight fans with the best possible entertainment.

The UFC's struggle for survival and turnaround was a testament to the indomitable spirit of its leadership and the passion of its fans. Despite facing numerous obstacles, Zuffa remained steadfast in its commitment to showcasing the sport's raw intensity while embracing regulations and safety measures.

The success of UFC 40, combined with Zuffa's strategic vision and television partnerships, catapulted the UFC onto a trajectory of continued growth and success. The organization had embarked on a journey of triumph, turning a struggling promotion into a global sporting phenomenon.

The Zuffa era would go on to produce some of the most memorable and historic moments in the history of mixed martial arts. The UFC's journey from the brink of bankruptcy to becoming a mainstream sensation was a testament to the enduring appeal of combat sports and the unwavering dedication of those who believed in its potential.

As the UFC's influence continued to grow, the struggle for survival and triumphant turnaround in the early 2000s would forever shape the organization's legacy, solidifying its place as a trailblazer in the world of sports and entertainment. The UFC had transcended its humble beginnings and was now firmly established as a global powerhouse, inspiring a new generation of athletes and fans alike. The UFC's success story served as a beacon of hope for combat sports enthusiasts worldwide, illustrating that with determination, vision, and unwavering commitment, anything is possible.

Chapter 6

The Ultimate Fighter and the Rise in Popularity - A Reality TV Revolution

As the Ultimate Fighting Championship (UFC) navigated through financial turmoil in the early 2000s, a groundbreaking idea would emerge, forever changing the trajectory of the organization. Faced with the prospect of folding, the UFC took a bold step outside the realm of pay-per-view and delved into the world of television. The brainchild of the Fertitta brothers, The Ultimate Fighter (TUF), a reality television show, would become the catalyst for the UFC's meteoric rise in popularity and establish the sport of mixed martial arts (MMA) as a cultural phenomenon.

Inspired by their earlier involvement in the reality television series American Casino, which proved to be an effective promotional tool, the Fertitta brothers conceived the idea of creating their own reality show centered around MMA fighters. The concept was simple yet revolutionary – pit up-and-coming fighters against each other in a competition for a coveted six-figure UFC contract. Elimination would occur through exhibition mixed martial arts matches, providing a real-life and unscripted portrayal of the challenges faced by aspiring fighters.

Although the Fertitta brothers believed in the potential of The Ultimate Fighter, the show faced rejection from several networks. Undeterred, they approached Spike TV with a unique offer – they would cover the entire $10 million production cost themselves. Recognizing the opportunity, Spike TV agreed to take a chance on the concept.

In January 2005, The Ultimate Fighter 1 made its debut on Spike TV, strategically scheduled to follow the popular WWE Raw programming. The show immediately struck a chord with viewers, captivating both MMA enthusiasts and a broader audience. The season culminated in a memorable finale, featuring a thrilling and intense brawl between light heavyweight finalists Forrest Griffin and Stephan Bonnar. Their unforgettable showdown for the six-figure contract became a defining moment for the UFC and The Ultimate Fighter.

The Impactful Success of The Ultimate Fighter

The first season of The Ultimate Fighter proved to be a resounding success, drawing considerable viewership and widespread attention. The live broadcast of the season finale achieved an impressive 1.9 overall rating, solidifying the show's place in mainstream culture. Dana White, the UFC's president, credits The Ultimate Fighter 1 with saving the organization from impending collapse. The momentum generated by the show's success was so profound that White allegedly negotiated the contract for the second season on a napkin immediately after the finale.

Building on the triumph of the inaugural season, subsequent seasons of The Ultimate Fighter were introduced in rapid succession, further propelling the UFC's popularity. The show's format of showcasing aspiring fighters battling for a shot at UFC stardom resonated with audiences, and fans eagerly tuned in to witness the raw emotions and intense competition inside the Octagon.

The collaboration with Spike TV extended beyond The Ultimate Fighter, as the network also aired UFC Unleashed, a weekly show featuring select fights from past events. Additionally, Spike broadcast live UFC Fight Night events starting in August 2005, and Countdown specials were developed to promote upcoming UFC pay-per-view cards. These initiatives provided a constant stream of UFC content, keeping fans engaged and fueling the sport's growth.

As the UFC's partnership with Fox was announced in August 2011, The Ultimate Fighter was poised for yet another transformative shift. Season 14 of the show would mark its last on Spike TV, and the UFC's flagship reality program would find a new home on FX.

Starting with season 15 in the spring of 2012, The Ultimate Fighter aired on Friday nights on FX. This move came with notable changes, such as episodes being edited and broadcast within a week of recording, eliminating the months-long delay experienced in previous seasons. Moreover, elimination fights were now aired live, adding a heightened sense of immediacy and excitement to the show.

The success of The Ultimate Fighter in the United States was quickly followed by the creation of international versions of the show. In 2009, The Ultimate Fighter: United Kingdom made its debut, featuring aspiring British fighters vying for a UFC contract. This expansion continued with The Ultimate Fighter: Brazil in 2012, followed by The Ultimate Fighter: China in 2014. The international editions not only introduced new talent to the UFC but also further solidified the organization's global footprint.

Throughout its multiple seasons, The Ultimate Fighter provided a platform for future UFC champions and top contenders. Notable fighters such as Michael Bisping, Rashad Evans, Nate Diaz, Tony Ferguson, and many others made their way into the UFC through the show. The Ultimate Fighter also produced some of the most iconic fights in UFC history, contributing to the organization's legacy of unforgettable moments.

In 2013, The Ultimate Fighter broke new ground by introducing a female bantamweight division for its 18th season. The season featured both male and female fighters living in the TUF house, marking the first time women were part of the show. This move further emphasized the UFC's commitment to promoting women's MMA and laid the groundwork for the eventual introduction of female UFC divisions.

The Ultimate Fighter's journey from an ambitious experiment to a television sensation is a testament to the power of innovation, determination, and unwavering belief in a vision. The show's remarkable impact on the UFC's resurgence and the rise of MMA as a mainstream sport is a legacy that continues to shape the sport's trajectory.

The Ultimate Fighter's revolutionary approach to blending competition and reality television has left an indelible mark on the sports and entertainment landscape. It showcased the resilience and talent of fighters while captivating audiences with emotional storylines and unforgettable battles inside the Octagon.

As the UFC's popularity soared and The Ultimate Fighter continued to captivate fans across the globe, the sport of MMA had firmly established itself as a force to be reckoned with in the world of sports and entertainment. The UFC's partnership with Spike TV and, later, Fox, enabled the organization to reach new heights, captivating millions of fans and solidifying its place as a global sporting phenomenon. The Ultimate Fighter had become a reality TV revolution, a true game-changer for the UFC and the sport of mixed martial arts. Its enduring legacy continues to inspire generations of fighters and fans, forever shaping the evolution of MMA as a globally celebrated sport.

Chapter 7

The Ultimate Fighter 1 Finale - A Night of Legends and Legendary Fights

The Ultimate Fighter: Team Couture vs. Team Liddell Finale marked a pivotal moment in the history of mixed martial arts (MMA) and the Ultimate Fighting Championship (UFC). Held on April 9, 2005, at the Cox Pavilion in Las Vegas, Nevada, the event showcased the finals from The Ultimate Fighter 1 reality show in both the middleweight and light heavyweight divisions. What was expected to be a mere prelude to the main event between UFC legend Ken Shamrock and rising star Rich Franklin turned into an unforgettable night of epic battles and iconic moments.

While the spotlight initially shone on the clash between Rich Franklin and Ken Shamrock, the ultimate surprise came from the light heavyweight finale. However, the main event still brought a fierce contest between two highly skilled fighters. In a bout that showcased both grappling and striking abilities, Rich Franklin emerged victorious, defeating the UFC Hall of Famer Ken Shamrock via technical knockout (TKO) in the first round. Franklin's impressive performance solidified his place as one of the top contenders in the light heavyweight division.

The Unforgettable Showdown: Forrest Griffin vs. Stephan Bonnar

While the main event was entertaining, it was the light heavyweight finale between Forrest Griffin and Stephan Bonnar that would steal the show and become a defining moment in UFC history. Both fighters had endured challenging paths to reach the finale, with controversial victories and hard-fought battles along the way. Despite their distinct fighting styles – Forrest's striking prowess and Stephan's jiu-jitsu expertise – the unexpected happened when Bonnar chose to engage in a toe-to-toe stand-up war with Griffin.

For three rounds, the electrifying atmosphere at the Cox Pavilion reached a fever pitch as Griffin and Bonnar exchanged strikes in a non-stop, back-and-forth war. The crowd erupted in raucous applause as they witnessed one of the greatest fights in MMA history. The judges awarded Forrest Griffin the unanimous decision victory (29–28, 29–28, 29–28), making him the first Ultimate Fighter winner in the light heavyweight division.

The Griffin vs. Bonnar fight had an unforeseen and profound impact on the UFC's future. The event's broadcast on Spike TV attracted an estimated three million viewers, resulting in a then-record 280,000 pay-per-view buys for the coaches' fight at UFC 52. Dana White, the UFC's president, often credited this epic battle as the driving force behind securing a second season of The Ultimate Fighter and propelling the UFC's popularity to new heights.

This remarkable fight and the subsequent TUF boom led to a surge in interest in MMA, both as a spectator sport and as a training discipline. The fight's display of heart, determination, and skill captured the imaginations of fans worldwide and highlighted the true essence of UFC fighters. The impact of this event was felt far beyond the Octagon, inspiring a new generation of fighters and enthusiasts to embrace the sport of MMA.

The legacy of the Griffin vs. Bonnar fight extended beyond its immediate impact. In recognition of their incredible performance and the significance of the bout, both Forrest Griffin and Stephan Bonnar were inducted into the UFC Hall of Fame in 2013. This accolade solidified the fight's place as one of the highlights of both fighters' careers and a seminal moment in UFC history.

The Ultimate Fighter: A Catalyst for Success

The Ultimate Fighter: Team Couture vs. Team Liddell Finale showcased the power of reality television in transforming the UFC into a cultural phenomenon. It proved that MMA could captivate mainstream audiences and that the sport's future was bright. The success of The Ultimate Fighter laid the groundwork for the UFC's continued rise in popularity and expansion into new markets.

The historic event at the Cox Pavilion demonstrated that the UFC was not just a combat sport but an entertainment spectacle capable of capturing the hearts of millions. The unforgettable battles and incredible performances on that fateful night solidified the UFC's place as a global sporting juggernaut. The Ultimate Fighter: Team Couture vs. Team Liddell Finale will forever be etched in MMA history as a night of legends and legendary fights, a turning point for the sport and the UFC's path to greatness.

The main event at The Ultimate Fighter 1 Finale featured a clash between two veteran fighters – Rich Franklin and Ken Shamrock. Both men were well-established names in the MMA world, with impressive careers behind them. Rich Franklin was riding a five-fight win streak in the UFC and was determined to solidify his place as a top contender in the light heavyweight division. On the other hand, Ken Shamrock, a UFC Hall of Famer and pioneer of the sport, was looking for a triumphant return to the Octagon after a stint in professional wrestling.

From the opening bell, it was evident that Franklin's striking skills and technical prowess were too much for Shamrock to handle. Franklin expertly landed a series of powerful punches and kicks, overwhelming Shamrock with his offensive display. As the first round progressed, Franklin's onslaught intensified, and Shamrock found himself trapped against the cage, unable to defend effectively.

In a thrilling climax, Franklin delivered a devastating knee strike, followed by a barrage of punches, leaving Shamrock battered and bloodied. Unable to mount any significant offense, Shamrock was unable to continue, and the referee stopped the fight, awarding Rich Franklin the TKO victory at 2:42 of the first round.

For Rich Franklin, the victory against a seasoned veteran like Ken Shamrock elevated his status in the UFC and set him on a path to challenge for the light heavyweight title. Meanwhile, Ken Shamrock's return to the Octagon proved to be a challenging endeavor, but his legacy as a pioneer and ambassador of the sport remained intact.

The Griffin vs. Bonnar Classic - A Turning Point for the UFC

As impressive as the main event was, it was overshadowed by the unforgettable showdown between Forrest Griffin and Stephan Bonnar in the light heavyweight finale. Both fighters had showcased their talents and heart throughout the season, but no one could have predicted the legendary fight that would unfold on that night.

Forrest Griffin, known for his never-say-die attitude and relentless striking, faced Stephan Bonnar, a jiu-jitsu expert with a solid stand-up game. While most expected a clash of styles, Bonnar surprisingly chose to stand and trade punches with Griffin from the opening bell. What followed was a three-round war that would go down in history as one of the greatest fights in MMA.

Griffin and Bonnar exchanged a barrage of strikes, showcasing incredible heart, resilience, and determination. Each fighter landed significant shots, pushing themselves to the limits of endurance. The crowd at the Cox Pavilion was on their feet, witnessing a display of true warrior spirit and sportsmanship.

When the final bell rang, both fighters had left everything inside the Octagon, and the judges had a difficult task ahead of them. In the end, Forrest Griffin was awarded the unanimous decision victory (29–28, 29–28, 29–28), becoming the first light heavyweight winner of The Ultimate Fighter.

However, the epic nature of the fight led to an unexpected decision by Dana White, the UFC's president. Recognizing the incredible heart and performance of both fighters, White offered Stephan Bonnar a UFC contract as well. This gesture spoke volumes about the significance of the fight and its impact on the sport.

The Griffin vs. Bonnar fight's impact extended far beyond The Ultimate Fighter 1 Finale. The broadcast of the fight on Spike TV attracted millions of viewers, and the ensuing pay-per-view event featuring coaches Chuck Liddell and Randy Couture set a then-record 280,000 buys. The success of The Ultimate Fighter 1 Finale marked the beginning of what is now known as "the TUF boom."

Interest in MMA skyrocketed, with more people tuning in to watch fights and participating in various martial arts disciplines. The iconic showdown between Griffin and Bonnar had touched the hearts of fans and inspired a new generation of fighters and enthusiasts. The UFC's popularity soared to unprecedented heights, and the sport of MMA had firmly established itself in mainstream culture.

Forrest Griffin and Stephan Bonnar: Hall of Fame Honors

In 2013, both Forrest Griffin and Stephan Bonnar were inducted into the UFC Hall of Fame in the "Fight" wing. Their epic battle at The Ultimate Fighter 1 Finale forever immortalized them as two of the sport's greatest warriors. Beyond their individual accomplishments in the sport, they will forever be remembered for the fight that changed the course of UFC history.

The Ultimate Fighter reality show continued to be a catalyst for the UFC's success. As it moved to FX in 2012 and subsequently to ESPN, it introduced new talent to the sport, produced numerous future champions, and captivated audiences with its captivating storytelling.

The Ultimate Fighter 1 Finale will forever be etched in the annals of MMA history as a night of legends and legendary fights. Rich Franklin's impressive victory over Ken Shamrock and the unforgettable showdown between Forrest Griffin and Stephan Bonnar solidified this event's place as a turning point for the UFC's rise in popularity. The impact of that night's battles, the TUF boom that followed, and the ongoing success of The Ultimate Fighter have left an indelible mark on the sport of MMA and continue to shape its future. The Ultimate Fighter: Team Couture vs. Team Liddell Finale was more than just an MMA event; it was a cultural phenomenon that changed the world of combat sports forever.

Chapter 8

Mid-2000s Expansion - The UFC's Rise to Mainstream Success

The mid-2000s marked a transformative period for the Ultimate Fighting Championship (UFC), as the organization experienced exponential growth and gained mainstream recognition. This chapter delves into the factors that fueled the UFC's expansion, the record-breaking pay-per-view buy rates, strategic acquisitions, and increased media coverage that propelled the UFC to new heights.

Pay-Per-View Boom and Record-Breaking Buy Rates

The turning point for the UFC came with the inception of The Ultimate Fighter reality show. The first season, which aired in 2005, pitted fighters from two teams coached by Randy Couture and Chuck Liddell against each other. The finale of the inaugural season featured a memorable showdown between Forrest Griffin and Stephan Bonnar. Hailed as one of the greatest fights in MMA history, their epic three-round stand-up war captivated viewers and showcased the heart and determination of UFC fighters.

The success of The Ultimate Fighter significantly increased the UFC's visibility, leading to a surge in pay-per-view buy rates. UFC 52, the first event after the inaugural season, headlined a rematch between Chuck Liddell and Randy Couture. This event drew a pay-per-view audience of 300,000 buys, doubling the previous benchmark set at UFC 40. The second season of The Ultimate Fighter further bolstered the UFC's popularity, with a main event between Liddell and Couture at UFC 57 attracting an estimated 410,000 pay-per-view buys.

Record-breaking pay-per-view buy rates became the norm for the UFC in the mid-2000s. UFC 60: Hughes vs. Gracie, featuring Royce Gracie's first UFC fight in 11 years, drew 620,000 buys, while UFC 61, headlined by the highly anticipated rematch between coaches Ken Shamrock and Tito Ortiz from The Ultimate Fighter 3, reached an impressive 775,000 buys. The pinnacle was reached with UFC 66, where Ortiz faced off against Liddell in a rematch, achieving over 1 million pay-per-view buys. This event solidified the UFC's status as a mainstream sports attraction and showcased the star power of its top fighters.

As the UFC's popularity continued to soar, the organization recognized the need to strengthen its executive team. In March 2006, the UFC hired Marc Ratner, the former executive director of the Nevada Athletic Commission, as Vice President of Regulatory Affairs. Ratner's experience and connections in the world of combat sports proved invaluable in the UFC's efforts to expand and gain acceptance in jurisdictions inside and outside the United States that had yet to sanction the sport.

Ratner, once an ally of Senator John McCain's campaign against "no holds barred" fighting, lobbied numerous athletic commissions to help raise the UFC's media profile and to push for the legalization of mixed martial arts in various regions. His expertise in navigating regulatory issues and gaining approvals played a crucial role in the UFC's expansion and acceptance as a legitimate sport.

Zuffa's Acquisitions: WEC and WFA

To solidify its position in the MMA landscape, Zuffa, the parent company of the UFC, made strategic acquisitions in late 2006. First, they acquired World Extreme Cagefighting (WEC), a promotion based in northern California that focused on showcasing lighter weight classes. This move allowed Zuffa to prevent the International Fight League (IFL) from making a deal with Versus (now NBC Sports Network) and expanded the UFC's reach into different weight divisions.

The acquisition of WEC not only brought the UFC new talent and weight classes but also helped showcase a broader range of fighters, catering to diverse fan interests. The lighter weight classes, with fighters who possessed speed, technical skills, and a penchant for exciting fights, further enriched the UFC's fight cards.

Additionally, Zuffa acquired the assets of World Fighting Alliance (WFA), a Las Vegas-based rival promotion. While WFA had signed notable fighters such as Quinton "Rampage" Jackson and Lyoto Machida, their events proved to be a financial disaster. Zuffa's acquisition of select assets from WFA, including fighter contracts and trademarks, further solidified the UFC's dominance in the MMA market.

The UFC's growing popularity extended beyond television viewership and attendance numbers. In July 2007, BodogLife.com, an online gambling site, declared that the UFC was set to surpass boxing for the first time in terms of betting revenues. The sports betting community recognized the potential and excitement that the UFC brought to the table.

With fans and bettors investing more than ever in the UFC, it became evident that the sport was capturing the attention of a wide audience. The UFC's rise as a major player in the sports entertainment industry was undeniable, and the organization's revenue streams were breaking records.

In fact, the UFC's financial success was nothing short of astonishing. In 2006, the organization generated over $222 million in pay-per-view revenue alone, surpassing both WWE and boxing. This remarkable achievement highlighted the UFC's appeal and demonstrated that it had evolved into much more than just a niche combat sport.

The UFC's success in the mid-2000s caught the attention of mainstream media outlets, providing additional exposure for the sport. In May 2007, Roger Huerta graced the cover of Sports Illustrated, a testament to the UFC's growing appeal. Additionally, Chuck Liddell's appearance on the front of ESPN The Magazine further solidified the sport's place in mainstream sports coverage.

The Ultimate Fighter reality show had not only revitalized the UFC but also opened doors for the organization in the mainstream media landscape. The UFC's fighters were becoming household names, and the sport was gradually shedding its previous stigma of being a brutal and underground spectacle.

The UFC's remarkable growth in the mid-2000s was the result of a perfect storm of factors. The popularity of The Ultimate Fighter, record-breaking pay-per-view buy rates, strategic acquisitions, and recognition by the betting community all contributed to the organization's ascent to mainstream success.

With each successful event, the UFC expanded its fan base, reaching new audiences and markets around the world. The promotion's willingness to embrace different weight classes, introduce new stars, and adopt innovative marketing strategies made it an attractive option for fans seeking thrilling and unpredictable sporting action.

The mid-2000s were a transformative period for the UFC, as the organization experienced exponential growth and gained mainstream recognition. The success of The Ultimate Fighter reality show, combined with record-breaking pay-per-view buy rates, strategic acquisitions, and increased media coverage, propelled the UFC to new heights. With a roster of charismatic fighters, strategic partnerships, and a growing fan base, the UFC cemented its position as a dominant force in sports entertainment, and its expansion into the mainstream market was just beginning. The mid-2000s expansion laid the foundation for the UFC's continued growth and emergence as a global sports phenomenon. The organization was ready to embrace the challenges and opportunities that lay ahead as it continued its journey to becoming one of the most prominent sports organizations in the world.

Chapter 9

Pride Acquisition and Integration - The Global Expansion of UFC

In Japan, Mixed Martial Arts (MMA) took a distinct and parallel evolution with origins in "shoot wrestling," a form of professional wrestling that emphasized realistic-looking moves and matches while downplaying theatrical elements. Promotions like Shooto and Pancrase had already begun organizing hybrid fighting shows with real fights by the time the UFC was founded, setting the stage for the creation of Pride Fighting Championships in 1997. At its peak, Pride became the world's most popular MMA promotion, playing a significant role in popularizing the sport both in Japan and around the globe. With large attendances in spacious sports arenas and millions of viewers through free-to-air and pay-per-view television, Pride helped solidify MMA's place as a major sporting spectacle.

The Rise and Fall of Pride Fighting Championships

Pride's success, however, faced a turning point in 2006 when it encountered financial difficulties following the termination of lucrative contracts with Japanese TV networks due to a scandal revealing deep ties between Pride and the Yakuza, Japan's notorious organized crime syndicate. The scandal tarnished the promotion's reputation and affected its ability to secure new television deals.

On March 27, 2007, a significant moment in MMA history occurred when the UFC and Pride announced an agreement in which the majority owners of the UFC, Frank and Lorenzo Fertitta, would purchase the Pride brand. This acquisition was seen as a landmark event that could potentially align two major MMA organizations and lead to co-promoted events featuring champions and top contenders from both organizations. Many drew comparisons to the merger of the AFL and NFL that led to the creation of the Super Bowl in American football.

Initially, there were intentions to run the organizations separately but in alignment. However, Dana White, the President of the UFC, quickly realized that the Pride model was not sustainable, especially in Japan where the brand had become "toxic" due to the scandal. The difficulties in securing a new television deal for Pride further reinforced the decision to integrate the two organizations.

Following the acquisition, the UFC made the strategic decision to fold the Pride organization, incorporating many of its top fighters into the UFC brand. This move brought iconic fighters such as Antônio Rodrigo "Minotauro" Nogueira, Maurício "Shogun" Rua, Dan Henderson, Mirko "Cro Cop" Filipović, Wanderlei Silva, and others under the UFC banner, strengthening the promotion's already talented roster.

The integration of Pride fighters into the UFC roster not only bolstered the promotion's talent pool but also created a sense of anticipation among fans, eager to witness dream matchups between fighters from both organizations. Fighters who once competed in Japan's Pride organization were now set to face off against UFC stalwarts, resulting in compelling and high-stakes fights.

With Pride's top fighters now part of the UFC roster, the promotion's global appeal soared to new heights. The UFC capitalized on the star power of these fighters, leveraging their popularity to draw attention to major events and increase pay-per-view buy rates. The integration of Pride fighters into the UFC also solidified the promotion's reputation as the premier MMA organization in the world.

Lorenzo Fertitta played a pivotal role in the UFC's international growth. In June 2008, he resigned from his position at Station Casinos to focus on the international business development of Zuffa, the parent company of the UFC. This move proved instrumental in expanding the UFC's reach to new territories.

Under Fertitta's guidance, the UFC struck television deals in China, France, Mexico, and Germany, effectively broadening its global viewership and fan base. Additionally, the promotion explored alternative revenue streams through licensing agreements, including the creation of a successful UFC video game and action figures, among other ventures.

The Legacy of Pride and the UFC's Global Dominance

Despite the dissolution of Pride, its legacy remains ingrained in the history of MMA. The promotion's contribution to the growth and popularity of the sport in Japan and worldwide cannot be overstated. Pride's unique blend of entertainment and competitive fighting left an indelible mark on the MMA landscape.

The acquisition of Pride by the UFC marked a significant turning point for the sport. It accelerated the UFC's global expansion and further solidified its position as the leading MMA organization. The addition of top Pride fighters to the UFC roster added to the promotion's appeal and paved the way for some of the most memorable fights in MMA history.

In conclusion, the acquisition and integration of Pride Fighting Championships by the UFC represented a pivotal moment in MMA history. The rise and fall of Pride showcased the sport's popularity in Japan and the potential for global expansion. The UFC's strategic move to incorporate top Pride fighters under its banner elevated its status as the premier MMA organization worldwide. With Lorenzo Fertitta's vision and leadership, the UFC capitalized on its international appeal, expanding into new markets and solidifying its position as a global sports phenomenon. The legacy of Pride lives on in the memories of fans, while the UFC continues to be at the forefront of MMA competition, shaping the future of the sport and captivating audiences around the world. As the UFC embraced its new status as a global powerhouse, the sport of MMA reached unprecedented heights, and its journey towards mainstream acceptance and success continued unabated.

Chapter 10

Late 2000s–Mid-2010s Growth with UFC 100 - The Rise of the UFC's Superstars and Record-Breaking Events

The late 2000s and mid-2010s marked a period of significant growth and popularity for the Ultimate Fighting Championship (UFC), driven by marquee events, charismatic fighters, and expanded media coverage. One pivotal moment during this era was UFC 100, a landmark event that showcased the drawing power of the promotion and set the stage for further success.

UFC's Popularity Surge with UFC 100

The UFC's popularity soared in 2009, fueled by a string of compelling events leading up to UFC 100. Events such as UFC 90, 91, 92, 94, and 98, alongside the anticipation for UFC 100, captured the attention of fight fans worldwide. Each event featured thrilling matchups and memorable performances from the sport's biggest stars, setting the stage for the grand spectacle that would be UFC 100.

UFC 100, in particular, was a resounding success, attracting an impressive 1.6 million pay-per-view buys. The main attractions included former NCAA wrestling and WWE Champion Brock Lesnar facing off against former UFC Heavyweight Champion Frank Mir in a highly anticipated rematch. Their heated rivalry and the aura surrounding Lesnar as a former professional wrestling superstar contributed to the immense interest in the fight. Additionally, Canadian superstar Georges St-Pierre squared off against Brazilian contender Thiago Alves in the co-main event. St-Pierre's widespread appeal and exceptional skills made him a fan-favorite and a major draw for the promotion. Another featured bout pitted American Dan Henderson against British rival Michael Bisping in a middleweight clash following their stints as rival coaches on The Ultimate Fighter: United States vs. United Kingdom. This matchup added an extra layer of anticipation and excitement to UFC 100, as the rivalry between the coaches spilled over into their bout inside the Octagon.

The significance of UFC 100 extended beyond just the event itself. It garnered extensive media coverage, drawing interest from major sports networks like ESPN, which provided pre- and post-event coverage. The exposure on ESPN led to increased attention and coverage of the UFC and other MMA news, ultimately leading to the television debut of the show "MMA Live" on ESPN2 in May 2010. The heightened media attention and coverage on mainstream sports networks played a crucial role in elevating the UFC's status and expanding its reach to a broader audience.

Despite the success of UFC 100, the promotion faced challenges in the second half of 2009. A series of injuries and health-related issues among fighters, including Brock Lesnar's life-threatening bout with diverticulitis, disrupted event lineups and forced the UFC to adapt and reshuffle its plans. The unpredictability of injuries and health issues in combat sports is a constant challenge for promotions, and the UFC's ability to pivot and find suitable replacements for marquee matchups demonstrated its resilience and commitment to providing exciting fights for fans.

Nevertheless, the organization's resilience allowed it to navigate these obstacles and continue to captivate audiences with thrilling matchups. The fight card shuffling, while initially disappointing for some fans, often led to unexpected and exhilarating showdowns. The willingness of fighters to step up on short notice to fill vacancies in the fight card further endeared them to the fans, as it demonstrated their dedication to the sport and their commitment to entertaining the audience.

The UFC's momentum picked up in the first quarter of 2010 with notable victories from defending champions Georges St-Pierre and Anderson Silva. St-Pierre's successful title defense against challenger Dan Hardy at UFC 111 solidified his position as one of the sport's pound-for-pound best. Meanwhile, Anderson Silva's dramatic come-from-behind submission victory over Chael Sonnen at UFC 117 remains one of the most memorable comebacks in MMA history. These victories solidified St-Pierre and Silva's status as dominant champions and added to the growing excitement around the sport.

Another notable event during this period was UFC 113, featuring a highly anticipated rematch between Maurício "Shogun" Rua and Lyoto Machida for the UFC Light Heavyweight title. Rua avenged his earlier loss to Machida and claimed the title, further establishing the competitive nature of the light heavyweight division and solidifying his status as one of the division's top contenders.

This period culminated in an exciting clash between former UFC Champions and rivals Rashad Evans and Quinton Jackson at UFC 114, featuring the UFC's first main event headlined by black fighters. The event garnered over 1 million pay-per-view buys and was a testament to the promotion's growing appeal and diverse fan base. The rivalry between Evans and Jackson, fueled by their stint as rival coaches on The Ultimate Fighter 10: Heavyweights, added an extra layer of drama and anticipation to the fight.

Summer of 2010: Brock Lesnar's Return and UFC 129

The summer of 2010 further bolstered the UFC's popularity with UFC 116, which featured Brock Lesnar's return to defend his UFC Heavyweight title against undefeated interim-champion Shane Carwin. Lesnar's dramatic victory over Carwin, surviving an early barrage of punches and ultimately submitting him via arm-triangle choke, showcased his star power and resilience. Lesnar's larger-than-life persona and reputation as a former WWE superstar continued to attract mainstream attention to the sport, further elevating the UFC's standing as a major player in the sports world.

The historic UFC 129 event took center stage in Toronto, Ontario, Canada, at the Rogers Centre. The event's main attraction was Georges St-Pierre's defense of his welterweight title against Jake Shields. The event is currently the largest in North American UFC history, an impressive feat that reflects the sport's growing popularity and international appeal. In addition to the record-breaking attendance, the event coincided with a two-day UFC Fan Expo at the Direct Energy Centre, showcasing the fervent fan base and community surrounding the sport.

One of the most significant milestones during this period was the UFC's first exhibition in New York City on November 5, 2016. The promotion overcame years of delays and bureaucratic hurdles to host the event, featuring a dramatic clash between Conor McGregor and Eddie Alvarez. This event marked a momentous achievement for the UFC as it finally secured its place in the sports capital of the world. The event generated immense buzz and excitement, drawing fans from around the world and further solidifying the UFC's position as a global sports phenomenon.

The late 2000s and mid-2010s marked a period of tremendous growth and success for the UFC. UFC 100 and the events leading up to it showcased the promotion's ability to draw massive audiences and generate record-breaking pay-per-view buys. The rise of charismatic fighters like Brock Lesnar, Georges St-Pierre, Anderson Silva, and Conor McGregor, among others, captured the imagination of fight fans worldwide. The UFC's ability to adapt to challenges, coupled with its resilience and dedication to delivering thrilling matchups, solidified its position as the premier MMA organization in the world. As the promotion expanded its global reach, hosted unprecedented events, and broke attendance and revenue records, it cemented its legacy as a driving force behind the growth and mainstream acceptance of mixed martial arts. The UFC's success in this era laid the groundwork for the organization to continue its ascent and evolve into the global sports powerhouse it is today.

Embark on a transformative journey through the eyes of one of MMA's greatest legends, Georges St-Pierre. "The Way of the Fight" offers not just a glimpse into the physical aspects of the sport but a profound exploration of mindset, discipline, and the essence of combat sports. Add this to your reading list for a unique perspective from a true martial arts icon.

Chapter 11

The WEC Merger - A New Era of Opportunity and Growth

In late 2006, Zuffa, the parent company of the Ultimate Fighting Championship (UFC), made a pivotal move by purchasing the World Extreme Cagefighting (WEC) promotion. This acquisition marked a significant step in the evolution of mixed martial arts (MMA) and set the stage for a groundbreaking merger that would change the landscape of the sport forever.

The Birth of WEC under Zuffa Ownership

Under Zuffa's ownership, the WEC held its first event on January 20, 2007. The move to the larger and more established Zuffa umbrella brought newfound visibility and resources to the WEC, enhancing its potential for growth. As a testament to its commitment to expanding the brand, the WEC entered into a partnership with the Versus Network, debuting its first event on that network in June 2007. This collaboration proved to be instrumental in the promotion's growth and further solidified its place in the MMA landscape.

Over the next few years, the WEC showcased some of the most electrifying and high-flying fighters in the sport. With a focus on the lighter weight classes, the WEC brought attention to divisions often overshadowed in other promotions. Talented fighters like Urijah Faber, José Aldo, Dominick Cruz, and Anthony Pettis emerged as stars, captivating audiences with their incredible skill sets and exciting fighting styles.

The WEC gained a reputation for consistently delivering thrilling fights and unforgettable moments. Its events featured fast-paced action and highlight-reel knockouts, captivating both hardcore MMA fans and casual viewers alike. As the promotion's popularity grew, it drew attention from media outlets and attracted an ever-increasing fan base.

On October 28, 2010, Zuffa made a historic announcement that reverberated throughout the MMA community. The WEC would merge with the UFC, bringing together two prominent promotions under one banner. The news sent shockwaves through the sport, sparking both excitement and speculation about the potential implications of the merger.

As part of the merger, the UFC absorbed WEC's bantamweight, featherweight, and lightweight divisions, along with their respective fighters. This move was significant as it provided a platform for the talented fighters from the lighter weight classes to compete on a bigger stage and gain exposure to a wider audience. The merger would also streamline the MMA landscape, creating a more cohesive structure for the sport and strengthening the UFC's position as the premier organization in MMA.

A New Beginning: UFC Champions and the Future of the WEC Fighters

With the merger, the last WEC Featherweight and Bantamweight Champions, José Aldo and Dominick Cruz, respectively, were crowned the inaugural UFC Champions in their respective weight divisions. This recognition was a testament to their skill and achievements in the WEC and marked a new beginning for these fighters as they transitioned to compete under the UFC banner.

The merger also offered opportunities for other WEC fighters to make their mark in the UFC. Many of the WEC's top talents were integrated into the UFC roster, providing them with a chance to showcase their abilities on the sport's biggest stage. This influx of new talent added depth and diversity to the UFC's roster, bolstering its appeal to fans worldwide.

As news of the merger spread, it elicited mixed emotions from those involved with the WEC. Reed Harris, who co-founded the WEC with Scott Adams, expressed a range of feelings when discussing the merger. He likened it to a parent seeing their child go off to college, initially feeling apprehensive but ultimately proud and happy for the opportunities that lie ahead. Harris, along with others who had been part of the WEC's journey, took pride in the promotion's growth and success and recognized that the merger with the UFC would elevate the sport to new heights.

For fighters like Urijah Faber, who had been a face of the WEC, the merger opened new doors and presented fresh challenges. Transitioning to the larger UFC stage meant facing new opponents and vying for a chance to become a UFC champion. Faber and other WEC veterans embraced the opportunity, eager to prove themselves against the best fighters in the world.

Impact on the Sport of MMA

The merger between the WEC and the UFC had a profound impact on the sport of MMA. By bringing the lighter weight classes under the UFC banner, it further solidified the organization's position as the premier destination for elite fighters and captivating matchups. Fans now had the opportunity to witness some of the most talented and dynamic fighters in the world competing on the biggest stage in MMA.

The merger also paved the way for significant growth in the lighter weight classes. As more attention and resources were focused on these divisions, they flourished, attracting a new generation of fighters and expanding the talent pool in the sport. The success of the merger also encouraged other promotions to prioritize the lighter weight classes, leading to the rise of flyweight and strawweight divisions in various organizations.

The WEC merger with the UFC represented a pivotal moment in the history of MMA. It not only united two influential promotions but also solidified the UFC's position as the leading organization in the sport. The merger allowed fighters from the WEC to compete on the grandest stage of MMA, offering them the chance to showcase their skills to a global audience. The integration of the lighter weight classes into the UFC brought a new level of excitement and talent to the promotion, further expanding the fan base and attracting new viewers. As the WEC's legacy became forever intertwined with the UFC, it marked the beginning of a new era of opportunity and growth for the sport of mixed martial arts. The WEC merger set the stage for future milestones and further solidified the UFC's status as the premier destination for the world's top fighters and the most thrilling MMA action. The impact of this historic merger continues to resonate in the sport of MMA to this day.

Chapter 12

The Strikeforce Purchase - A New Chapter in MMA History

On March 12, 2011, the mixed martial arts (MMA) world was abuzz with news that would forever change the landscape of the sport. Dana White, the president of Zuffa, made a groundbreaking announcement that his company had acquired Strikeforce, a prominent MMA promotion known for showcasing top-tier talent and delivering thrilling fights. This acquisition marked a turning point in the history of both organizations and opened the door to a new chapter in MMA history.

A Rising Star: The Legacy of Strikeforce

Founded in 1985 as a kickboxing promotion, Strikeforce evolved into an MMA promotion in 2006 under the leadership of Scott Coker. From its inception, Strikeforce sought to differentiate itself by featuring a diverse roster of fighters, with a particular emphasis on showcasing female fighters—an area where other promotions were lagging behind. Under Coker's guidance, Strikeforce quickly gained recognition as a premier promotion, earning a loyal fan base and attracting top talent from around the world.

Strikeforce's rise to prominence was fueled by its ability to produce compelling matchups and deliver high-quality events. The promotion consistently delivered exciting fights that captivated audiences, earning a reputation for its competitive divisions and thrilling title bouts. Strikeforce also distinguished itself by fostering talent in various weight classes, contributing to the growth and development of MMA as a whole.

One of the defining moments in Strikeforce's history came in 2009 when they signed a landmark deal with Showtime to broadcast their events. This partnership with a major cable network helped elevate Strikeforce's profile and reach a broader audience. As a result,

Strikeforce events gained more exposure and became a staple for MMA enthusiasts worldwide.

With Zuffa's acquisition of Strikeforce, the MMA landscape underwent a seismic shift. Zuffa, the parent company of the Ultimate Fighting Championship (UFC), was already the dominant force in the MMA world, and the addition of Strikeforce further solidified its position as the industry leader. The move was met with both excitement and speculation as fans and fighters alike wondered how the two organizations would integrate and what the future would hold.

Dana White's announcement assured fans that Strikeforce would continue to operate as an independent promotion, with Scott Coker at the helm. This commitment to maintaining Strikeforce's identity was met with approval from many fans who appreciated the unique flavor that Strikeforce brought to the sport. Moreover, the continuation of co-promotional efforts with M-1 Global signaled a willingness to collaborate and create opportunities for cross-promotional events, adding further intrigue to the partnership.

The acquisition also raised questions about potential talent exchanges and super-fights between the UFC and Strikeforce champions. Fans eagerly speculated about dream matchups that had previously been confined to the realm of fantasy. The possibilities were endless, and anticipation grew as the MMA world eagerly awaited what the future would hold for both promotions.

One of the early announcements following the acquisition was the return of Fedor Emelianenko, a legendary heavyweight fighter and one of the sport's most iconic figures. Fedor's presence in Strikeforce added star power to the promotion and further fueled anticipation for future events. Fans eagerly awaited his comeback, wondering which formidable opponents he would face in the Strikeforce cage.

Fedor's return to Strikeforce was met with both excitement and intrigue. The enigmatic Russian heavyweight had built a reputation as one of the most dominant fighters in MMA history, boasting an impressive undefeated streak that spanned nearly a decade. His signing with Strikeforce opened the door to potential dream matchups with top UFC heavyweights, igniting the imagination of fight fans around the world.

Additionally, the merger brought significant changes to the heavyweight division. The Strikeforce Heavyweight Grand Prix had been a marquee event for the promotion, attracting attention from fans and pundits alike. While the finalists would not join the UFC, the rest of the division merged into the UFC. This move infused the UFC's heavyweight division with fresh talent and opened up new possibilities for exciting matchups.

The End of an Era: Strikeforce's Final Show

Despite the initial excitement and optimism surrounding the merger, all good things must come to an end. On January 12, 2013, Strikeforce held its final event, Strikeforce: Marquardt vs. Saffiedine. The event marked the end of an era for the promotion, as it bid farewell to its fans and fighters who had been an integral part of its success.

The final Strikeforce event was a bittersweet moment for the MMA community, as it represented the closing of a chapter in the sport's history. It provided an opportunity for reflection on the memorable moments, thrilling fights, and unforgettable fighters who had graced the Strikeforce cage over the years. As the promotion took its final bow, fans and fighters alike expressed gratitude for the impact it had made on the sport and the opportunities it had provided to athletes to showcase their talents on a global stage.

Following the event, the promotion was officially dissolved, and fighter contracts were either terminated or absorbed into the UFC. While the end of Strikeforce was bittersweet, its impact on the sport of MMA would forever be remembered. Many of the promotion's fighters, including Ronda Rousey and Daniel Cormier, would go on to achieve great success in the UFC, further solidifying Strikeforce's legacy as a talent-rich breeding ground for MMA stars.

A New Chapter in MMA History

The acquisition of Strikeforce by Zuffa marked a significant moment in MMA history, one that would shape the future of the sport for years to come. The partnership between two of the industry's powerhouses offered exciting possibilities for cross-promotional events, dream matchups, and opportunities for fighters to compete on the biggest stage in MMA.

While the chapter of Strikeforce came to a close, its legacy would live on through the fighters who had made their mark in the promotion and the unforgettable moments that had captured the hearts of fans worldwide. The merger with Zuffa further solidified the UFC's position as the dominant force in MMA, and Strikeforce's unique contributions to the sport would forever be etched in its history.

As MMA continued to grow and evolve, the acquisition of Strikeforce served as a testament to the sport's increasing global appeal and the boundless potential for future growth. With the UFC at the helm, MMA was poised for a new era of unparalleled excitement, talent, and innovation, with Strikeforce's legacy serving as a guiding light for the stars of tomorrow. The story of the Strikeforce purchase would forever be enshrined in the annals of MMA history, a reminder of the sport's ability to unite, evolve, and conquer new frontiers. As fans looked to the future, they did so with a sense of anticipation and wonder, eager to witness the next chapter of MMA's extraordinary journey.

Chapter 13

The Fox Partnership - A New Era of MMA Broadcasting

On August 18, 2011, the mixed martial arts world witnessed a groundbreaking announcement that would forever change the landscape of MMA broadcasting. The Ultimate Fighting Championship (UFC) and Fox, a prominent television network, unveiled a historic seven-year broadcast deal that would revolutionize how MMA events were showcased to audiences worldwide. The partnership marked a significant milestone in the sport's journey to mainstream recognition and solidified the UFC's position as a global powerhouse in combat sports.

The Birth of the Fox Partnership

For years, the UFC had been steadily building its reputation as the premier MMA promotion in the world. Under the leadership of Dana White and the Fertitta brothers, the promotion had experienced unprecedented growth, drawing in millions of fans and generating record-breaking pay-per-view buy rates. As the sport's popularity soared, the UFC sought to expand its reach and deliver its electrifying fights to an even wider audience.

Fox, one of the most prominent television networks in the United States, had been keenly observing the rise of MMA and recognized its potential as a major draw for sports enthusiasts. Seeing an opportunity to tap into the rapidly growing MMA market, Fox made a bold move to secure a partnership with the UFC. The result was a groundbreaking seven-year broadcast deal that would forever change the trajectory of MMA broadcasting.

The Terms of the Deal

The Fox-UFC partnership was a multifaceted agreement that brought together the promotional prowess of the UFC and the broadcasting reach of Fox Sports. The deal included several key components that promised to elevate the sport to new heights:

Broadcast Events: The partnership promised to deliver four major UFC events each year on the main Fox network. These events would feature high-profile fights and marquee matchups, providing millions of viewers with an opportunity to witness the excitement of MMA on broadcast television.

Live Friday Night Fights: As part of the agreement, Fox committed to airing 32 live Friday night fights per year on its cable network FX. These weekly events would showcase up-and-coming talent and provide fans with a consistent dose of live MMA action.

The Ultimate Fighter Integration: The popular reality show, The Ultimate Fighter (TUF), was also set to become a significant part of the partnership. Following each season of TUF, the UFC would host 24 live events, further bolstering its presence on the Fox Sports platform.

Fight Night Events: Additionally, the deal included six separate Fight Night events, adding even more opportunities for fans to enjoy live MMA action.

The Landmark Debut: UFC on Fox: Velasquez vs. dos Santos

The debut event under the Fox partnership was nothing short of historic. Dubbed UFC on Fox: Velasquez vs. dos Santos, the event took place on November 12, 2011, and set a new standard for MMA broadcasting. Unlike traditional pay-per-view events that featured multiple fights, this broadcast focused solely on one high-stakes matchup.

In the main event, reigning UFC heavyweight champion Cain Velasquez faced off against the heavy-hitting Brazilian, Junior dos Santos. The highly anticipated clash promised fireworks, and it delivered in spectacular fashion. In a stunning upset, dos Santos scored a first-round knockout, abruptly dethroning the previously undefeated champion.

The numbers were equally impressive. The telecast peaked with a staggering 8.8 million viewers tuning in for the bout, with an average audience of 5.7 million. This made it not only the most-watched MMA event of all time but also the most-watched combat sports event since the 2003 HBO bout between Lennox Lewis and Vitali Klitschko.

A New Era of MMA Broadcasting

The success of UFC on Fox: Velasquez vs. dos Santos set the tone for the future of MMA broadcasting under the Fox partnership. The collaboration between the UFC and Fox Sports proved to be a winning formula, bringing the sport to a broader audience and cementing its place in mainstream sports entertainment.

With regular live events on Fox Sports platforms, including FX and the main Fox network, MMA became more accessible than ever before. The weekly Friday night fights on FX allowed fans to follow the rise of promising fighters and witness the next generation of MMA stars in the making.

Furthermore, the UFC's continued production control ensured that the sport's authenticity and excitement remained at the forefront of each broadcast. Longtime commentators Mike Goldberg and Joe Rogan continued to provide insightful commentary, enhancing the viewing experience for MMA enthusiasts.

The success of the Fox partnership extended beyond the events themselves. The agreement also created opportunities for additional programming, including a weekly magazine-style show that offered behind-the-scenes insights, fighter profiles, and highlights from recent events. This further immersed fans in the world of MMA and helped build a deeper connection between fighters and their audience.

The Fox partnership not only elevated MMA's presence in the United States but also played a crucial role in expanding the sport's global reach. The UFC's live events and programming were now accessible to viewers around the world through Fox's extensive international network of channels. This global exposure enabled the UFC to gain a significant foothold in international markets and introduced MMA to new audiences on a global scale.

The Growth of The Ultimate Fighter

As an integral part of the Fox partnership, The Ultimate Fighter continued to be a driving force in MMA's mainstream appeal. The reality show had already enjoyed several successful seasons on Spike TV, but the move to Fox Sports provided a broader platform for the show's reach. Each season of The Ultimate Fighter showcased promising talent, with aspiring fighters competing for a coveted UFC contract.

The show's innovative format and dramatic storytelling captivated both hardcore MMA fans and new viewers alike. With behind-the-scenes footage, intense training sessions, and the emotional journey of each fighter, The Ultimate Fighter became a must-watch for MMA enthusiasts and casual sports fans alike.

The Fox partnership also had a profound impact on the careers of MMA fighters. The increased exposure and larger audience meant that fighters had the opportunity to elevate their profiles and gain more significant recognition. This newfound visibility not only led to higher paydays for fighters but also opened doors to lucrative sponsorship deals and other business opportunities outside the Octagon.

Additionally, the partnership brought a new level of professionalism and production value to MMA events. Each broadcast was meticulously produced, highlighting the UFC's commitment to delivering top-notch entertainment to its growing fanbase.

The Fox partnership left an indelible mark on the sport of MMA and played a pivotal role in its journey to mainstream recognition. The groundbreaking broadcast deal showcased the UFC's ability to reach a wider audience and solidify its position as a leading force in sports entertainment.

Over the course of the partnership, countless memorable moments and legendary fights graced the Fox Sports platform. From jaw-dropping knockouts to epic title showdowns, the partnership delivered non-stop action and excitement to fans around the globe.

As the partnership continued to thrive, it also opened the door for other sports networks and media outlets to take note of MMA's growing popularity. The success of the Fox deal inspired other major networks to explore partnerships with MMA promotions and further contributed to the sport's mainstream acceptance.

While the Fox partnership eventually came to an end, its legacy continues to resonate within the MMA community. It set the stage for future broadcasting deals and collaborations, showcasing the enduring appeal of MMA as a global phenomenon.

As the UFC continues to evolve and expand its reach, the Fox partnership will always be remembered as a pivotal moment in the sport's history. It was a time when MMA secured its place among the most-watched and beloved sports in the world, and its influence continues to shape the future of combat sports broadcasting. As the sport of MMA continues to grow and captivate audiences, the Fox partnership remains a testament to the unwavering dedication and passion of fighters, promoters, and fans alike.

Chapter 14

Women's MMA: Breaking Barriers and Shaping a New Era

The inclusion of women's mixed martial arts (MMA) in the UFC was a groundbreaking moment that marked a significant shift in the sport's landscape. Prior to this historic development, women's MMA had been thriving in smaller promotions like Strikeforce and Invicta Fighting Championships, but it had yet to receive the recognition and platform it deserved on the world stage.

The Rise of Ronda Rousey and the Birth of Women's UFC

The pivotal moment came on November 16, 2012, when UFC President Dana White announced that the promotion would feature women's MMA. The catalyst for this decision was the signing of none other than Ronda Rousey, the Strikeforce bantamweight champion and a dynamic force in the sport. Rousey's impressive fighting skills, combined with her charisma and outspoken nature, made her a perfect candidate to lead the charge for women's MMA in the UFC.

As the first female UFC fighter, Ronda Rousey went on to achieve an incredible list of "firsts" in her career. She became the inaugural UFC women's bantamweight champion, breaking barriers and shattering glass ceilings for women in the sport. Rousey's dominance inside the Octagon was unparalleled, and she quickly became one of the most recognizable and influential figures in MMA.

Her Impact on Women's MMA

Ronda Rousey's success in the UFC had a profound impact on the perception and acceptance of women's MMA. Her star power and marketability helped to dispel the notion that women's fights were somehow inferior or less entertaining than men's bouts. Rousey's fights were eagerly anticipated by fans of all genders, and her performances delivered the high-level action and excitement that MMA fans craved.

Beyond her accomplishments in the cage, Rousey's impact extended to the UFC's business and promotional strategies. With

Rousey at the forefront, the UFC put more resources and promotional efforts into women's fights, recognizing the market potential and drawing power of female athletes. This newfound emphasis on women's MMA opened doors for other talented female fighters to shine on the big stage.

The Strawweight Division and The Ultimate Fighter

With the success of Ronda Rousey and the growing interest in women's MMA, the UFC expanded its offerings by creating the 115-pound strawweight division. In December 2013, the UFC purchased the contracts of 11 female fighters from Invicta Fighting Championships to bolster this new division. Notable fighters like Carla Esparza, Rose Namajunas, and Joanna Jędrzejczyk were among those signed, adding depth and talent to the roster.

To introduce the strawweight division to the masses, the UFC took an innovative approach. Eight of the newly signed fighters, along with eight others who earned their spot through open tryouts, were featured in the 20th season of The Ultimate Fighter (TUF). The reality show provided a platform for these fighters to showcase their skills and build their reputations, culminating in a tournament that would determine the inaugural UFC women's strawweight champion.

Carla Esparza emerged as the victor, defeating Rose Namajunas in the finale to become the first-ever UFC women's strawweight champion. The success of The Ultimate Fighter: Team Pettis vs. Team Melendez not only provided the UFC with an exciting new champion but also solidified the strawweight division as a mainstay in the promotion.

The Expansion of Women's MMA Worldwide

As the popularity of women's MMA continued to soar, the UFC's international expansion included a focus on showcasing female fighters in various locations around the globe.

Canada was an early adopter of women's MMA, hosting events that featured female fighters competing at the highest level. UFC 186, held in 2015, was the most recent event in Canada, underscoring the country's support for women's MMA.

In the United Kingdom, women's MMA also found a welcoming audience. UFC 70 marked the promotion's return to the UK in 2007, and since then, female fighters have been regularly featured in events held in the region.

Brazil, a hotbed of MMA talent, had its first taste of women's UFC action at UFC Brazil: Ultimate Brazil in 1998. The promotion did not return to Brazil until 2011 for UFC 134, but since then, the country has hosted a further 20 events. Their most recent visit was UFC Fight Night: Condit vs. Alves.

The rise of women's MMA in Latin America was equally notable, with Mexico becoming the second country in the region to host a UFC event in 2014. The promotion's expansion into Mexico and other Latin American countries opened doors for talented fighters from the region to showcase their skills on a global stage.

The UFC's foray into Asia presented new opportunities for women's MMA to thrive. Countries like Japan, the United Arab Emirates, Macau, Singapore, and the Philippines have all hosted UFC events, featuring female fighters from their respective regions.

In addition to its domestic editions, The Ultimate Fighter introduced international versions, providing female fighters from different countries with a platform to showcase their talent. Editions in Brazil, Australia, China, Canada, and Latin America allowed these fighters to compete on a global stage and connect with fans worldwide.

The success of these international editions further solidified the global appeal of women's MMA. Female fighters from diverse backgrounds and cultures found their place in the sport, proving that talent knows no borders.

The Legacy of Women's MMA

The inclusion of women's MMA in the UFC and its subsequent global expansion has left an indelible mark on the sport. Today, female fighters are an integral and celebrated part of the MMA landscape, with champions like Amanda Nunes, Valentina Shevchenko, and Weili Zhang leading the way.

The legacy of women's MMA extends far beyond the Octagon. Female fighters have become role models for young athletes, proving that dedication, skill, and determination know no gender. Their accomplishments have inspired a new generation of female fighters to pursue their dreams and break down barriers in sports.

As women's MMA continues to grow and thrive, its presence on the global stage will undoubtedly continue to expand. With each new event and championship bout, female fighters will continue to captivate audiences worldwide and redefine what it means to be a champion in the world of mixed martial arts. The evolution of women's MMA is a testament to the resilience and determination of female athletes, as well as the ongoing commitment of the UFC and the broader MMA community to embrace diversity, equality, and excellence in the sport.

The Emergence of Female Superstars

The rise of women's MMA brought with it a new generation of female superstars who captured the hearts of fans and pushed the boundaries of what was possible inside the Octagon.

Amanda Nunes, known as "The Lioness," stands as one of the most dominant champions in UFC history. Her thunderous knockout victories over legends like Ronda Rousey and Cris Cyborg solidified her status as a force to be reckoned with in both the bantamweight and featherweight divisions. Nunes became the first woman in UFC history to hold two titles simultaneously, a testament to her unparalleled skill and versatility as a fighter.

Valentina Shevchenko, often referred to as "Bullet," quickly established herself as a fierce competitor in the flyweight division. With a background in Muay Thai and a lethal striking game, Shevchenko displayed precision and technical prowess in her performances, earning her a spot as one of the most formidable champions in her weight class.

Weili Zhang, also known as "Magnum," brought the intensity of Chinese martial arts to the UFC and quickly became a fan favorite. Her epic showdown with Joanna Jędrzejczyk at UFC 248 showcased her heart, determination, and unyielding spirit, making her a role model for aspiring fighters across the globe.

The success of women's MMA transcended the world of sports, igniting conversations about gender equality and female empowerment. Female fighters like Ronda Rousey and Miesha Tate played critical roles in challenging stereotypes and proving that women could excel in combat sports.

These fighters not only inspired young girls to pursue their dreams but also brought greater visibility to issues such as pay parity and opportunities for women in male-dominated industries. Their stories of resilience, dedication, and triumph resonated with audiences worldwide, prompting discussions about breaking barriers in all aspects of life.

The Future of Women's MMA

The journey of women's MMA is far from over. As the sport continues to evolve, so does the talent pool of female fighters. New contenders emerge, each seeking to leave their mark on the sport and claim championship gold.

The UFC's commitment to women's MMA remains steadfast, evidenced by the ever-expanding divisions and the promotion's ongoing efforts to showcase female fighters on high-profile fight cards. Events like International Women's Day Fight Night celebrate the contributions of women in the sport and create a platform to amplify their voices.

Beyond the Octagon, female fighters have embraced their roles as ambassadors for change and empowerment. They use their platforms to advocate for causes close to their hearts and inspire others to pursue their passions fearlessly.

The inclusion of women's MMA in the UFC and its subsequent growth on the global stage have forever changed the landscape of mixed martial arts. Through the dedication and talent of female fighters, the sport has evolved into a more inclusive and diverse community, breaking barriers and inspiring generations to come. As the legacy of women's MMA continues to unfold, its impact on the world of sports and beyond will undoubtedly leave a lasting mark on the hearts and minds of millions around the world.

Dive into the compelling autobiography of a trailblazer in women's MMA. Ronda Rousey's "My Fight / Your Fight" not only chronicles her remarkable journey to the top but serves as an empowering narrative for anyone chasing their dreams. A must-read for fight enthusiasts and those inspired by tales of resilience.

Chapter 15

The TRT Ban: A Turning Point in MMA's Drug Testing and Anti-Doping Efforts

The Controversy Surrounding TRT in MMA

The use of Testosterone Replacement Therapy (TRT) in mixed martial arts (MMA) had been a contentious and controversial issue for years, with debates about its fairness, safety, and impact on competition. TRT is a medical treatment that involves the use of synthetic testosterone to treat individuals with abnormally low levels of the hormone. The therapy is intended to help patients alleviate symptoms associated with low testosterone, such as fatigue, reduced muscle mass, and decreased libido.

However, in the world of MMA, TRT became a controversial issue when some fighters started to exploit the therapy to gain a competitive advantage. Athletes using TRT argued that they needed the treatment to bring their testosterone levels back to normal after years of wear and tear from training and fighting. They claimed that the therapy was a medical necessity, allowing them to maintain their physical and mental health while continuing to compete at the highest level.

The Controversy Grows: Accusations of Doping and Unfair Advantage

As the use of TRT in MMA gained prominence, accusations of doping and unfair advantage started to surface. Critics argued that TRT was simply a legal form of doping, allowing fighters to gain an unfair advantage over their opponents. Fighters with exemptions for TRT were legally allowed to use synthetic testosterone, giving them a competitive edge over opponents who were not using the treatment.

Prominent fighters like Chael Sonnen, Vitor Belfort, and Dan Henderson, who had exemptions for TRT, faced criticism and suspicion from both fans and fellow fighters. Many questioned the legitimacy of their performances and achievements, raising concerns about the integrity of the sport. This controversy reached its peak when several TRT-using fighters tested positive for banned substances, further fueling the debate over the fairness of the treatment.

Calls for Change: Public Outcry and Fighter Opposition

As public awareness of TRT use in MMA grew, so did the calls for change. Fans and media outlets criticized the system that allowed fighters to use TRT, arguing that it undermined the integrity of the sport and created an uneven playing field. MMA organizations, particularly the UFC, faced mounting pressure to address the issue and take decisive action.

Fighters, media personalities, and anti-doping advocates voiced their opposition to TRT use in MMA. Some fighters, like Michael Bisping, openly accused TRT users of cheating and called for stricter drug testing in the sport. Others, including former champions like Georges St-Pierre, expressed concerns about the impact of TRT on fighter safety and the potential for abuse.

The Decision to Ban TRT: Nevada State Athletic Commission Takes Action

In the face of mounting public outcry and growing concerns about TRT's impact on the sport, the Nevada State Athletic Commission (NSAC) took the lead in initiating change. On February 27, 2014, the NSAC made a momentous decision that would send shockwaves through the MMA community: they banned the use of TRT in combat sports.

The NSAC's decision to ban TRT marked a significant turning point in the fight against performance-enhancing drugs in MMA. It sent a clear message that the use of synthetic testosterone for performance enhancement would no longer be tolerated in the sport. The decision was met with both praise and criticism from fighters, fans, and industry experts, reflecting the divisive nature of the issue.

The UFC's Response: Implementing a Ban on TRT

Following the NSAC's decision, the UFC quickly followed suit and implemented its own ban on TRT for all events under their jurisdiction. The ban applied not only to events held in the United States but also to international markets where the UFC oversaw regulatory efforts. This move was significant as it demonstrated the promotion's commitment to clean and fair competition across the board.

The UFC's decision to ban TRT was widely praised by fans, fighters, and anti-doping advocates who saw it as a crucial step towards a cleaner and more reputable sport. The ban marked a turning point in the promotion's drug testing and anti-doping efforts, signaling its willingness to address the issue of performance-enhancing drugs in MMA.

The World Anti-Doping Agency (WADA) played a crucial role in shaping the UFC's anti-doping efforts, including the TRT ban. WADA is a global organization dedicated to promoting, coordinating, and monitoring the fight against doping in sports. Their anti-doping code sets the international standard for drug testing in sports and is adopted by various sports organizations, including the UFC.

The UFC's adoption of WADA's anti-doping policies and procedures demonstrated its commitment to aligning with global standards and best practices in the fight against doping. The UFC partnered with the United States Anti-Doping Agency (USADA) to implement a comprehensive and rigorous drug testing program, ensuring that fighters were subject to random testing throughout their careers.

The Introduction of Year-Round Testing: A New Era of Clean Competition

The introduction of the UFC's anti-doping program, which included year-round testing and stringent penalties for drug violations, marked a significant shift in the promotion's approach to drug testing.

It demonstrated the UFC's dedication to maintaining the integrity of the sport and protecting the health and safety of its athletes.

With year-round testing by USADA, fighters were subject to random testing at any time, whether in or out of competition. This increased scrutiny and deterrence helped to level the playing field and restore confidence in the legitimacy of MMA competition. The UFC's commitment to clean competition became a defining characteristic of the promotion, setting a new standard for drug testing in combat sports.

The Legacy of the TRT Ban: A Safer and Fairer Sport

The TRT ban and the subsequent anti-doping efforts in MMA are a testament to the sport's commitment to progress and its willingness to confront challenges head-on. By taking a proactive approach to drug testing and clean competition, MMA has positioned itself as a leader in the fight against doping in sports.

As the sport continues to evolve, the legacy of the TRT ban serves as a reminder of the importance of upholding the values of fairness, respect, and sportsmanship in MMA. By maintaining a commitment to clean competition and rigorous drug testing, the sport of MMA can continue to thrive and inspire the next generation of fighters and fans alike.

A Turning Point in MMA's Drug Testing and Anti-Doping Efforts

The TRT ban represented a pivotal moment in the history of MMA. It brought issues of fairness, integrity, and athlete safety to the forefront of the sport's consciousness. The ban and the subsequent anti-doping efforts by the UFC demonstrated a commitment to clean competition and set a new standard for drug testing in MMA.

As the sport of MMA continues to grow and gain mainstream popularity, its commitment to clean competition and rigorous drug testing will remain paramount. By upholding the values of fairness, respect, and sportsmanship, MMA can continue to thrive as a legitimate and respected sport on the global stage. The TRT ban served as a catalyst for change and set the stage for a new era of clean and fair competition in mixed martial arts.

Chapter 16

Lawsuits over Contractual Treatment of Fighters

In the ever-evolving world of mixed martial arts (MMA), the treatment and compensation of fighters have been subjects of intense scrutiny and legal battles. This chapter delves into significant lawsuits that have shaped the landscape of fighter rights and contractual agreements within the industry.

In December 2014, a seismic shift occurred in the MMA world when several fighters filed an antitrust lawsuit against Zuffa, the parent company of the UFC. The lawsuit alleged that Zuffa engaged in anticompetitive practices that limited fighters' control over their careers and earning potential, effectively monopolizing the industry. This landmark case, which took place in the Nevada federal court, sparked debates and discussions about fighter rights, earning potential, and the power dynamics within the sport.

Fighter Pay Disparities and Revenue Sharing

As the antitrust lawsuit progressed, an alarming issue emerged—the vast disparity in fighter pay compared to other major sports leagues. While the NBA, MLB, and NHL typically share approximately half of their revenue with their athletes, the UFC was estimated to share only between 16% and 22% of its revenue with fighters. Advocates for fighter rights argued that the UFC's long-term exclusive contracts and "champion's clauses" were tactics designed to suppress fighter pay and restrict their ability to negotiate with other promotions. This issue ignited heated debates within the MMA community, with fighters and their representatives calling for increased revenue sharing and fairer distribution of profits.

The Cung Le and Nate Quarry Lawsuit of 2020

The fight for fair treatment and better pay continued with another significant lawsuit filed in 2020 by a group of fighters led by Cung Le and Nate Quarry. This lawsuit alleged that the UFC violated antitrust laws by engaging in anti-competitive practices that kept fighter pay artificially low. The plaintiffs claimed that the UFC's practice of using long-term exclusive contracts and "champion's clauses" was intended to suppress fighter pay and prevent them from negotiating with other promotions. They also alleged that the UFC engaged in other anti-competitive practices, such as blocking fighters from using their own image and likeness rights and taking a significant portion of revenue from merchandise sales. Despite facing challenges, the fighters' determination to seek justice resulted in a revival of the case by the appeals court in 2021.

In yet another impactful lawsuit, former fighter Leslie Smith took on the UFC, challenging the classification of fighters as independent contractors instead of employees. Smith argued that this classification violated federal labor laws and deprived fighters of certain benefits and protections afforded to employees. Her case aimed to shed light on the need for fair treatment and recognition of fighters' rights within the MMA industry. Although the case was initially dismissed in 2019, Smith's unwavering determination led to an appeal, keeping the fight for fighter rights alive.

Continuing the Fight for Fighter Rights and Fair Treatment

The lawsuits over the contractual treatment of fighters have sparked a movement for change within the MMA industry. They have brought attention to the need for increased transparency, fair revenue sharing, and a reevaluation of fighter contracts. As the journey towards a more equitable and just MMA landscape continues, fighters, advocates, and industry stakeholders stand united in their pursuit of a sport that values and respects its athletes above all else.

The vision of a more inclusive and fighter-centric MMA industry inspires hope and determination, driving the community to work towards a brighter and more equitable future for all involved. The outcomes of these lawsuits and the resulting reforms have the potential to shape the future of MMA, elevating the sport to new heights of integrity and fairness. The pursuit of a more inclusive and fighter-centric MMA industry remains ongoing, with the collective goal of creating a sport that upholds the rights and well-being of its athletes above all else. As the sport continues to evolve, these lawsuits serve as reminders that the fight for fighter rights is not just a legal battle but a cultural shift that empowers athletes and fosters a more just and supportive environment within the world of MMA.

Chapter 17

The 2016 Sale to WME-IMG and a New Era

In May 2016, the mixed martial arts world was abuzz with rumors and speculation surrounding the potential sale of the Ultimate Fighting Championship (UFC). Reports emerged from ESPN, hinting at negotiations that could see the UFC's parent company, Zuffa, LLC, change hands for a staggering $3.5 billion to $4 billion. The mere possibility of such a deal sent shockwaves through the combat sports community, igniting discussions about the future of the sport, its fighters, and the potential impact on the global MMA landscape.

Amidst swirling rumors, potential buyers emerged, adding intrigue to the already captivating narrative. Notable entities like Dalian Wanda Group, China Media Capital, and the well-known entertainment and talent agency, WME-IMG (Endeavor), were reportedly among the interested parties. As fans and industry insiders eagerly awaited official confirmation, the UFC and its President, Dana White, remained tight-lipped, further fueling the intrigue and anticipation surrounding the potential sale.

Months passed, and finally, on July 9, 2016, the monumental announcement arrived. The UFC was officially sold to a consortium led by WME-IMG for an astonishing $4.025 billion, marking a historic moment in the world of sports. This acquisition represented the most substantial ever in sports history, highlighting the increasing value and popularity of mixed martial arts on a global scale.

The consortium consisted of major players in the financial and entertainment sectors, with Silver Lake Partners, Kohlberg Kravis Roberts, and MSD Capital joining forces with WME-IMG to take ownership of the UFC. Flash Entertainment, an entity owned by the government of Abu Dhabi, also retained its 10% minority stake in the company, showcasing the global appeal and diverse investor interest in the sport.

Throughout the acquisition process, Dana White's role remained a focal point of interest. As a pivotal figure in the UFC's meteoric rise, White chose to stay on board and retain his position as the President of the organization. Additionally, he retained a 9% ownership stake in the new entity, signifying the importance of his continued involvement in guiding the UFC's future direction.

With the sale complete, WME-IMG saw an opportunity to leverage the UFC's immense global appeal and expand its reach into new markets and territories. In September 2017, WME-IMG underwent a rebranding and adopted the name Endeavor, symbolizing the beginning of a new era for both the organization and the sport of mixed martial arts.

This transition into the Endeavor era marked a critical phase in the UFC's evolution. Under new ownership, the UFC aimed to capitalize on its popularity, secure lucrative broadcasting deals, and forge commercial partnerships that would further elevate the sport's status and reach. As the MMA landscape continued to evolve, industry stakeholders, fighters, and fans were eager to witness how the UFC's new owners would shape the sport's future.

Furthermore, the post-acquisition financial landscape of the UFC demonstrated remarkable growth and success. A financial report obtained by MMAJunkie indicated that in 2015, the promotion achieved a record-high revenue of $609 million. The report revealed that 76% of the total revenue was attributed to "content," which included media rights, pay-per-view buys, and subscriptions to the UFC Fight Pass platform. Notably, pay-per-view buys accounted for 42% of the content revenue, underscoring the significance of this revenue stream in the UFC's financial success.

As the UFC continued its journey under Endeavor's leadership, the organization made strategic moves to expand its global footprint. Endeavor recognized the importance of venturing into untapped markets, holding events in new countries, and establishing its presence in regions where MMA had yet to reach its full potential.

While the acquisition marked a turning point for the UFC, it also brought its share of challenges. Critics voiced concerns about the potential impact on fighters' earnings and working conditions. Some fighters raised questions about the fairness of contracts and revenue-sharing models. These concerns led to legal disputes and class-action lawsuits, highlighting the ongoing struggle for fair treatment and representation of fighters within the organization.

Notably, in 2020, a group of fighters led by Cung Le and Nate Quarry filed a lawsuit against the UFC, alleging that the promotion engaged in anti-competitive practices that suppressed fighter pay and limited their opportunities to negotiate with other promotions. The case sparked heated debates and discussions about fighter welfare and the need for further reforms within the sport.

Despite these challenges, the UFC continued to thrive under Endeavor's ownership. The promotion explored new ventures, including the expansion of the women's divisions and the establishment of Performance Institutes in various locations, aimed at providing fighters with state-of-the-art training facilities and support.

As the UFC ventured into new territories and secured broadcasting deals with major networks, its global popularity soared. The organization cultivated a dedicated fan base worldwide, transcending cultural boundaries and making stars out of fighters from diverse backgrounds.

The 2016 sale to WME-IMG ushered in a new era for the UFC, underscoring its status as a premier global sports organization. As Endeavor set its sights on further growth and international expansion, the UFC's place in the sports world was solidified. The acquisition served as a catalyst for the sport's continued development, innovation, and evolution, leaving the mixed martial arts community eager to witness the next chapter in the remarkable journey of the Ultimate Fighting Championship.

Chapter 18

The Reebok Uniform Deal: A New Era for UFC Fighters

In December 2, 2014, the Ultimate Fighting Championship (UFC) and Reebok made waves in the combat sports world by announcing an exclusive six-year partnership. Reebok would become the worldwide outfitter for the UFC, starting in July 2015. The deal represented a significant milestone for both organizations, marking the most valuable non-broadcast contract ever signed by the UFC. While financial details were not disclosed, the agreement was structured to ensure that the majority of the revenue from the deal would go directly to UFC fighters, signaling a new era in fighter compensation and branding.

A Pioneering Partnership

The announcement of the Reebok uniform deal signified a paradigm shift in the way fighters were outfitted and compensated in the UFC. With Reebok's renowned brand and global presence, the partnership promised to elevate the fighters' profiles and create a unified and professional image for the sport. Reebok's commitment to quality and innovation aligned seamlessly with the UFC's pursuit of excellence, making it a strategic alliance that captured the attention of fans and stakeholders alike.

The deal not only impacted the fighters' apparel but also extended to various aspects of their brand representation. The exclusive nature of the partnership meant that Reebok would become the sole provider of fight kits and apparel, ensuring a consistent and recognizable look for all UFC athletes. As part of the deal, fighters were given the option to choose between a universal kit and a country kit, representing their nationality. Additionally, a special champion kit was reserved exclusively for title holders, adding an extra layer of prestige to their status within the organization.

Evolution of Fighter Compensation

One of the most groundbreaking aspects of the Reebok uniform deal was the innovative approach to fighter compensation. Traditionally, fighters had relied on individual sponsorships to generate income and support their careers. However, with the introduction of the Reebok deal, the landscape of fighter compensation underwent a significant transformation.

Initially, the payment system was intended to be based on fighters' rankings in the official UFC rankings, with champions being excluded from the tiered structure. The plan was to pay fighters in four tiers based on their rankings, with the higher-ranked athletes receiving higher compensation. This structure aimed to reward fighters for their accomplishments and rankings within their respective divisions.

However, in April 2015, the UFC made the decision to revamp the payment system. Instead of basing compensation on rankings, fighters' pay would now be determined by the number of bouts they had in the octagon. This approach acknowledged the dedication and experience of fighters, compensating them based on their time and effort spent competing in the UFC. Different tiers were established, with fighters falling into categories based on the number of fights they had participated in.

Controversies and Adjustments

Despite the promising vision of the Reebok uniform deal, it was not without its share of controversies and criticisms. One of the main points of contention was the removal of existing sponsors from fighter clothing and in-cage sponsor banners. This change meant that fighters would no longer be able to display their individual sponsors during fight week and media appearances, leading to concerns about the potential loss of income for fighters who heavily relied on sponsorships.

Additionally, the elimination of third-party logos from UFC broadcasts, apart from title-sponsor slots, raised questions about the overall impact on fighter branding and sponsor visibility. While the deal aimed to create a uniform look and elevate the UFC's presentation, some believed that individual fighter identities could be overshadowed in the process.

To address these concerns, the UFC made efforts to strike a balance between the Reebok deal and fighters' individual sponsorships. While the Reebok uniform remained a prominent feature, the organization welcomed existing sponsors to continue supporting UFC fighters. Special arrangements were made for title-sponsor slots, allowing for potential partnerships with major global brands in the future.

Embracing the Uniform Identity

Despite the initial challenges and adjustments, many fighters and fans eventually embraced the uniform identity introduced by the Reebok deal. The cohesive look on fight nights and during media appearances created a sense of professionalism and unity among the athletes. Fighters expressed their appreciation for the high-quality Reebok gear and the recognition it brought to their achievements within the octagon.

Moreover, the royalty program for fighter merchandise sales provided an additional stream of income for fighters, especially those with a strong fan base. This program extended even to retired fighters, ensuring that their contributions to the sport would continue to be recognized and rewarded.

Looking Towards the Future

As the Reebok uniform deal continued to shape the UFC's identity, the partnership laid the foundation for future collaborations and innovations. The unified and professional appearance of fighters during events and media engagements strengthened the UFC's brand presence, elevating its status in the global sports market.

The evolution of fighter compensation also opened the door to further discussions on fair and equitable pay for fighters. While the system was not without flaws, it prompted dialogue about the value of fighters' contributions to the sport and their financial well-being.

As the UFC and Reebok explored new opportunities and fine-tuned the partnership, the future held endless possibilities for both organizations. With each fight, the Reebok uniform became a symbol of a fighter's dedication and commitment to their craft, reflecting the heart and soul they poured into their journey inside the octagon.

In the years to come, the Reebok uniform deal would continue to evolve, responding to the needs and feedback of fighters and fans alike. As the UFC's brand presence and global reach expanded, the partnership with Reebok would remain at the forefront of innovation, setting new standards for athlete representation and compensation in the world of combat sports. Together, the UFC and Reebok forged a path of excellence, leaving an indelible mark on the history of the sport and the fighters who proudly donned the Reebok uniform.

Chapter 19

The ESPN Partnership: A New Era of UFC Broadcasting

A Pioneering Deal in the World of Sports

In May 2018, the Ultimate Fighting Championship (UFC) embarked on a groundbreaking new chapter in its broadcasting history with the announcement of a momentous media rights deal. The UFC, in collaboration with Disney Direct-to-Consumer and International and ESPN Inc., entered into transformative partnerships that would shape the future of mixed martial arts (MMA) broadcasting. This monumental move signaled the UFC's ambition to elevate the sport to unprecedented heights, forging a strong alliance with one of the most influential media conglomerates in the world.

The five-year contracts, valued at an astounding $300 million per year, marked a significant increase in value compared to the UFC's previous deal with 21st Century Fox. This financial milestone not only demonstrated the surging popularity of the UFC but also underscored its position as a major player in the sports entertainment industry. With a cumulative worth of over $1.5 billion, the deal sent a resounding message that MMA had firmly secured its place in the global sports landscape.

A core aspect of the partnership was the inclusion of 42 events annually on ESPN platforms. This comprehensive coverage ensured that fight fans across the United States had access to a multitude of live UFC events on ESPN's various channels and digital platforms. From thrilling Fight Night events to the high-stakes drama of UFC pay-per-view cards, ESPN became the go-to destination for MMA enthusiasts seeking top-tier action and entertainment.

The partnership between the UFC and ESPN went beyond just broadcasting marquee events. ESPN's linear networks also played a vital role in the deal by televising preliminary cards for UFC pay-per-view events. This move allowed fans to experience the excitement of the build-up to the main card, ensuring that the anticipation leading up to the featured bouts was captured for viewers worldwide.

A Digital Revolution: UFC on ESPN+

Perhaps the most groundbreaking aspect of the collaboration was the prominence of ESPN+, the network's subscription streaming service. ESPN+ emerged as a digital powerhouse, broadcasting 20 exclusive UFC events per year under the branding UFC on ESPN+ Fight Night. This move was a game-changer, as it catered to the growing trend of digital streaming, allowing MMA enthusiasts to enjoy the sport's top-notch action through the convenience of online streaming.

The exclusive UFC on ESPN+ Fight Night events promised fans a full, 12-fight card, ensuring an action-packed evening of non-stop excitement. From the first preliminary bout to the final main event, fans were treated to a spectacle of skill, athleticism, and heart, making each event a memorable experience for fight enthusiasts.

The partnership granted ESPN+ on-demand rights to the extensive UFC library and archive content. This vault of MMA history allowed fans to delve into the rich heritage of the sport, reliving classic moments and epic battles. From legendary title fights to unforgettable submissions, fans could explore the sport's storied past, further fueling their passion for MMA.

In addition to the wealth of live events, ESPN+ secured new seasons of Dana White's Contender Series, a show that offered aspiring fighters a chance to showcase their skills and earn a coveted UFC contract. This unique opportunity gave rising talents a platform to prove their worth, making each episode a captivating journey of determination and ambition.

UFC Fight Pass, the UFC's digital streaming service dedicated to MMA content, found a home on ESPN+. By offering UFC Fight Pass as an add-on option for ESPN+ subscribers, fans were given even more flexibility to access premium UFC content, including pay-per-view events, creating an all-in-one streaming destination for UFC enthusiasts.

The Two-Year Extension and PPV Shift

Just one year into the partnership, ESPN and the UFC solidified their commitment to each other with a two-year extension of their contract. This demonstrated the success of the collaboration and the alignment of both parties' goals in furthering the growth and global impact of MMA.

The extension came with a pivotal shift in the way UFC pay-per-view events were accessed in the United States. Future UFC PPVs would now be exclusively sold through ESPN+ to its subscribers, marking the end of traditional television providers selling PPV events. This strategic move not only catered to the digital shift in media consumption but also made UFC events more accessible and affordable for fans.

Embracing the Digital Age: A Win-Win Partnership

The ESPN partnership ushered in a new era of broadcasting for the UFC, firmly establishing the sport as a global phenomenon. With ESPN's extensive reach and commitment to delivering top-notch sports content, the UFC's fan base continued to expand, captivating audiences worldwide. The marriage between the UFC and ESPN represented a win-win partnership, solidifying the UFC's position at the pinnacle of the sports entertainment landscape and propelling the sport of MMA into an exciting and prosperous future.

Chapter 20

The M-1 Global Partnership: Forging Connections in the World of Russian MMA

In a move that sent seismic ripples through the global MMA community, the Ultimate Fighting Championship (UFC) announced a groundbreaking partnership with M-1 Global, a prominent Russian MMA promoter, on July 18, 2018. This strategic alliance marked a significant milestone for both organizations, opening doors to new opportunities and solidifying their foothold in the Russian market. With Russia emerging as a hotbed for MMA talent, the collaboration provided the UFC with an unprecedented conduit to access and recruit the best fighters from the region, creating an exciting avenue for fighters to reach the pinnacle of their careers.

M-1 Global as the UFC's Russian Talent Pool

At the heart of the partnership was M-1 Global's pivotal role as a talent pool for the UFC, enabling the promotion to scout and discover promising Russian fighters. With Russia showcasing an abundance of skilled martial artists, the collaboration presented the UFC with a direct pipeline to tap into this wealth of untapped potential. The deep-rooted connections within the Russian MMA scene afforded M-1 Global a unique advantage in identifying and nurturing emerging talent, making it an ideal partner for the UFC's quest to bolster its roster with formidable athletes from the East.

The strategic agreement forged between the UFC and M-1 Global established the latter as an official farm league for the UFC, a visionary move aligned with the UFC's grand vision for global expansion. By serving as a stepping stone to the world's premier MMA organization, M-1 Global offered aspiring Russian fighters a clear and compelling path to the grand stage of the UFC. This symbiotic relationship not only benefited the fighters, providing them with a once-in-a-lifetime opportunity to showcase their skills to a global audience, but also strengthened the UFC's talent pool with a fresh influx of skilled and hungry athletes.

Beyond talent scouting, M-1 Global played an instrumental role in organizing UFC events within Russia's vast territory. With the Russian market proving to be an enthusiastic and receptive audience for MMA, the UFC seized the opportunity to host thrilling events on Russian soil, further solidifying its global reach. These landmark events not only catered to the passionate local fanbase but also served as a beacon of MMA's ever-growing popularity, captivating viewers worldwide with memorable battles within the Octagon.

A Gateway for M-1 Champions

A highly alluring aspect of the partnership was the pathway it provided for M-1 Global champions to transition into the UFC. As part of the groundbreaking deal, M-1 champions were presented with a direct opportunity to sign with the UFC, offering them a ticket to the grand stage where their skills and determination could shine on a global scale. This enticing incentive served as a powerful motivation for M-1 champions to push their limits and pursue excellence in their MMA journeys, driving them to new heights of achievement.

The collaboration between the UFC and M-1 Global transcended national boundaries, becoming a catalyst for international growth in the sport of MMA. By tapping into the talent-rich Russian market, the partnership represented a strategic move to expand the global reach and influence of MMA. This synergistic alignment brought fighters and fans from diverse cultures and backgrounds together, uniting them under the banner of mixed martial arts, fostering camaraderie, and celebrating the spirit of competition.

The UFC's partnership with M-1 Global presented an enticing opportunity to shine a spotlight on the meteoric rise of Russian MMA. With a host of top-tier fighters hailing from Russia, the collaboration offered a platform for these athletes to showcase their skills and dedication to the sport, leaving an indelible impression on fans worldwide. As the world watched, Russian fighters left an indelible mark on the international stage, adding a new layer of excitement and dynamism to the global MMA landscape.

The Evolution of Russian MMA

The partnership between the UFC and M-1 Global signified a momentous step in the evolution of Russian MMA. As the sport continued to gain traction and fervent popularity in the country, the collaboration provided essential support for its growth and development. With the UFC's vast resources and expertise, combined with M-1 Global's deeply rooted presence in Russia, MMA in the region experienced an unprecedented surge in popularity and recognition, carving its place as a cornerstone in the nation's sporting fabric.

Beyond immediate gains, the UFC's partnership with M-1 Global represented an investment in the future of MMA. By cultivating and nurturing Russian talent, the collaboration ensured a steady influx of skilled fighters into the global MMA arena, cementing the sport's future as a force to be reckoned with. This strategic foresight demonstrated the UFC's commitment to the long-term growth and sustainability of the sport, creating an enduring legacy for MMA in Russia and beyond.

The partnership between the UFC and M-1 Global stood as a testament to the power of collaboration in the world of sports. By uniting two influential organizations, each with its unique strengths and expertise, the MMA community witnessed the emergence of a dynamic and transformative alliance. This pioneering spirit set a new precedent for cooperation in the MMA landscape, inspiring further partnerships and fueling the sport's global ascent, serving as an inspiration for a new era of cooperation and synergy.

The Impact Unfolds

As the partnership between the UFC and M-1 Global continued to unfold, its profound impact was felt across the MMA landscape.

From the growth of Russian MMA to the global reach of the UFC's events, the collaboration forged an enduring legacy that would resonate throughout the annals of MMA history. As fighters from diverse backgrounds converged in the Octagon, MMA enthusiasts worldwide reveled in the excitement and spectacle that this historic alliance had unleashed. The journey had only just begun, and the MMA community eagerly anticipated the next chapter in the UFC and M-1 Global's shared pursuit of excellence.

Chapter 21

The Impact of the COVID-19 Pandemic on the UFC

An Unprecedented Challenge

As the COVID-19 pandemic swept across the globe, the sports world found itself facing an unprecedented challenge. The Ultimate Fighting Championship (UFC), one of the world's premier MMA organizations, was no exception. The pandemic brought about a series of disruptions, forcing the UFC to navigate uncharted waters and make tough decisions to safeguard the health of fighters, staff, and fans while ensuring the continuity of the sport. This chapter delves into the significant impact of the pandemic on the UFC, from event cancellations and venue changes to the emergence of "Fight Island" and the ensuing controversies.

As COVID-19 cases escalated worldwide, the UFC grappled with the dilemma of proceeding with scheduled events or prioritizing public safety. On March 13, 2020, the UFC held its event, UFC Fight Night: Lee vs. Oliveira, in Brasília, Brazil, behind closed doors as a first attempt to adapt to the new reality. However, in the ensuing days, the gravity of the situation prompted the organization to take more decisive actions. On March 16, it was announced that the next three events—UFC Fight Night: Woodley vs. Edwards, UFC on ESPN: Ngannou vs. Rozenstruik, and UFC Fight Night: Overeem vs. Harris—would be postponed to future dates.

The decision to postpone events had widespread ramifications, affecting not only fighters and fans but also the entire MMA ecosystem. Fighters faced uncertainties surrounding their training schedules and fight opportunities, while fans were left disappointed by the absence of live events. Additionally, the postponement of events had financial implications for the UFC and its stakeholders, with revenue streams from ticket sales, broadcasting rights, and sponsorships drying up.

The Saga of UFC 249

One of the most contentious chapters in the UFC's pandemic saga centered around UFC 249, scheduled for April 18, 2020. As cities went into lockdown, UFC president Dana White expressed his determination to stage the event, albeit behind closed doors. Initially slated for Barclays Center in New York, the event faced multiple hurdles, including a stay-at-home order and withdrawal of sanctioning by the New York State Athletic Commission. Undeterred, White explored alternative venues and even teased the concept of a "Fight Island" to host international fighters.

The saga of UFC 249 encapsulated the complexities of balancing sporting pursuits with public health concerns. White's determination to proceed with the event showcased the UFC's commitment to providing fans with a sense of normalcy during trying times. However, the controversies surrounding the event underscored the challenges of operating in a pandemic-stricken world, where the safety and well-being of fighters, staff, and the wider community were at stake.

The Rise of "Fight Island"

In a bold and innovative move, White revealed plans to secure a private island—dubbed "Fight Island"—to host events involving international fighters amidst travel restrictions. This concept generated immense buzz within the MMA community, capturing the imagination of fans and fighters alike. The promise of "Fight Island" symbolized the UFC's determination to overcome pandemic-induced obstacles and continue delivering riveting fights to audiences worldwide.

The emergence of "Fight Island" marked a turning point for the UFC, signifying its adaptability and creativity in navigating the pandemic landscape. By providing a secure location for international fighters to compete, the UFC addressed logistical challenges and showcased its commitment to global representation in the sport. The island's picturesque setting and unique concept further elevated the

UFC's brand and reinforced its status as a pioneering force in the MMA world.

With the UFC's determination undeterred, UFC 249 found its new venue at the Tachi Palace, a tribal casino in Lemoore, California. The tribal land status provided a loophole, allowing events to be self-sanctioned outside the jurisdiction of the California State Athletic Commission. As the UFC proceeded with plans to host UFC 249 at Tachi Palace, controversy ensued as ESPN and The Walt Disney Company intervened, leading to the event's cancellation, along with the suspension of all other UFC events.

The decision to host UFC 249 at Tachi Palace exemplified the lengths to which the UFC was willing to go to ensure the sport's continuity. However, the cancellation of the event underscored the delicate balance between the desire to provide entertainment and the need to prioritize public health. The intervention by media rightsholders and corporate stakeholders illustrated the complex interplay between sports, business, and public safety during the pandemic.

The Return of UFC with Precautionary Measures

Amid ongoing uncertainties, the UFC found a glimmer of hope when Florida declared professional sports as "essential services." Capitalizing on this opportunity, the UFC successfully held UFC 249 at VyStar Veterans Memorial Arena in Jacksonville, Florida, on May 9, 2020. The event took place without fans in attendance, with stringent precautionary health and safety measures in place, satisfying the Florida State Boxing Commission's requirements.

The return of UFC events with precautionary measures exemplified the organization's commitment to adapting to the evolving pandemic situation. The implementation of rigorous health protocols, such as regular testing, social distancing, and restricted access, showcased the UFC's dedication to creating a safe environment for all involved. The decision to proceed with events behind closed doors, while not ideal for fans, allowed the sport to continue its operations during challenging times.

Ronaldo Souza's COVID-19 Positive Test

Despite the meticulous precautions, the pandemic's impact still managed to reach the UFC's doorstep. Middleweight fighter Ronaldo Souza tested positive for COVID-19 ahead of his scheduled bout with Uriah Hall at UFC 249. Souza, along with his cornermen, were immediately quarantined, raising concerns about the potential risks involved in holding live events during the pandemic.

Souza's positive test highlighted the unpredictability of the pandemic's spread and its ability to infiltrate even the most stringent safety measures. The incident also sparked debates over the appropriateness of proceeding with events, as well as the need for constant vigilance and responsiveness in navigating the pandemic landscape.

Controversial UFC 261 and Public Health Concerns

As the pandemic persisted into 2021, the UFC hosted UFC 261 at VyStar Veterans Memorial Arena in Jacksonville, Florida, with a 100% sold-out capacity. This decision drew criticism from public health experts who cited concerns about the risks to attendees and the wider community. The event proceeded without mask mandates, reigniting debates over the appropriateness of hosting large-scale gatherings during the ongoing pandemic.

The controversies surrounding UFC 261 raised fundamental questions about the balance between entertainment and public health. While the UFC's desire to bring back live events and engage with fans was understandable, the potential risks posed by large gatherings remained a topic of intense scrutiny. The episode also sparked broader discussions about the role of sports in society during a global crisis.

The COVID-19 pandemic presented the UFC with an unprecedented challenge, pushing the organization to adapt, innovate, and make difficult decisions in a rapidly evolving landscape. From event cancellations to the emergence of "Fight Island" and the resumption of events with precautionary measures, the UFC demonstrated resilience and determination to continue providing fans with thrilling MMA action. However, the pandemic also brought to the forefront complex issues surrounding public health and safety, underscoring the need for cautious and responsible decision-making in the pursuit of normalcy in extraordinary times. As the world grappled with uncertainty, the UFC's journey through the pandemic became a testament to the power of adaptability and the enduring spirit of MMA. The lessons learned during this challenging period will undoubtedly shape the UFC's future, as it continues to navigate uncharted waters and strive to deliver exhilarating fights to its global audience.

Chapter 22

The Venum Uniform Deal: A New Era of Style and Partnership in the UFC

The partnership between the Ultimate Fighting Championship (UFC) and Venum was a highly anticipated and groundbreaking moment for both the mixed martial arts community and the combat sports apparel industry. Venum, renowned for its high-quality gear and stylish designs, stepped into the octagon as the exclusive outfitting partner of the UFC, beginning in April 2021.

Fighters and fans alike were excited to witness how Venum would infuse its unique flair and identity into the fighter uniforms. With a reputation built on delivering top-notch performance apparel for combat sports athletes, Venum's entry into the UFC marked a significant shift from the previous Reebok uniform, which had been in place since 2015.

The Debut of Venum Outfits

The much-awaited moment arrived in April 2021 when UFC on ABC: Vettori vs. Holland became the historic event that showcased the first-ever Venum outfits in the octagon. As the fighters made their way to the center of the arena, anticipation was high to witness the fresh and vibrant look that Venum had designed for them.

The debut of Venum outfits was met with enthusiasm from fighters, who appreciated the gear's comfort, durability, and functionality. Meticulously crafted to meet the demands of elite athletes, the Venum uniforms provided the necessary support and freedom of movement required for peak performance during their high-stakes bouts.

Section 3: The Avex Brasil Partnership

In October 2021, the UFC unveiled another exciting development in relation to the Venum uniform deal. The organization announced its strategic partnership with Avex Brasil, the local producer of Venum brand apparel, to serve as the exclusive manufacturer and distributor of

UFC Replica Fight Kits and Fight Week apparel sold through retailers in Brazil.

The collaboration with Avex Brasil represented a significant step towards catering to the passionate Brazilian audience, one of the UFC's biggest fan bases. By creating officially licensed UFC replica fight kits and fight week apparel specifically tailored for the Brazilian market, the partnership sought to deepen the connection between Brazilian fans and the sport they cherished.

The Impact of Venum's Style

The introduction of Venum outfits brought an unparalleled burst of style and individuality to the UFC. Venum's designs were a testament to the dynamic nature of the sport, capturing the essence of each fighter's unique identity. Notably, the Venum fight kits not only showcased the fighters' names and nationalities but also allowed for personalization and customization, empowering the athletes to express their personalities through their apparel.

The Venum uniform quickly became a symbol of unity and strength, representing the shared passion and dedication of fighters from around the world. Beyond the octagon, it resonated with fans, who embraced the new era of fighter uniforms with enthusiasm and admiration for Venum's artistic vision.

Throughout its partnership with the UFC, Venum remained steadfast in honoring the fighter spirit. The brand recognized the immense dedication, hard work, and sacrifice that went into each fighter's journey and was determined to create gear that celebrated their unwavering commitment to their craft.

Beyond mere apparel, the Venum uniforms became a source of inspiration for aspiring fighters and combat sports enthusiasts. The iconic Venum logo came to embody the spirit of martial arts and the relentless pursuit of excellence, inspiring a new generation of athletes to chase their dreams with unwavering determination.

A Future of Innovation and Collaboration

As the Venum uniform deal continued to unfold, the UFC and Venum looked towards a future of relentless innovation and fruitful collaboration. The partnership aimed to push boundaries, exploring new possibilities to elevate the fighter experience and engage fans on a deeper, more immersive level.

Venum's design team worked hand-in-hand with the UFC to create uniforms that were not just functional but also artistic masterpieces. The fight kits served as a canvas for artistic expression, with each fighter's walkout attire being a powerful statement of their character and values. Venum and the UFC remained committed to evolving the designs and technology, ensuring that fighters were equipped with gear that enhanced their performance while embodying their unique personas.

The Venum uniform deal was truly transformative, marking a significant turning point in the history of the UFC. The partnership between the UFC and Venum brought together two forces of excellence, united in their commitment to celebrating the fighter spirit and elevating the sport of mixed martial arts. As fighters stepped into the octagon, clad in Venum's bold and stylish gear, they embodied the essence of combat sports - fierce, determined, and unyielding in the pursuit of victory. With Venum's commitment to innovation and the UFC's dedication to delivering the best fighting experience, the partnership promised a future of endless possibilities and continued growth in the world of MMA.

Chapter 23

Controversy Over Eye Pokes in the UFC

The sport of mixed martial arts (MMA) has witnessed significant advancements in safety measures over the years, aimed at protecting fighters from potential injuries. However, one contentious issue that continues to plague the Ultimate Fighting Championship (UFC) is the occurrence of eye pokes during fights. Eye pokes, accidental or otherwise, can have severe consequences, leading to eye injuries, fight stoppages, and heated debates about fighter safety. This chapter explores the controversies surrounding eye pokes in the UFC, the calls for change, and the ongoing efforts to address this persistent safety concern.

The Incident at UFC Fight Night: Edwards vs. Muhammad

In March 2021, the UFC was thrust into the spotlight over the issue of eye pokes following a crucial incident at UFC Fight Night: Edwards vs. Muhammad. During the final bout of the event, a severe eye poke suffered by Leon Edwards resulted in the fight being halted, raising serious questions about the potential risks posed by the standard UFC gloves. The incident ignited a firestorm of debate, as fighters, trainers, and commentators voiced their concerns about the need for enhanced fighter safety measures.

The incident at UFC Fight Night: Edwards vs. Muhammad brought the issue of eye pokes to the forefront, prompting widespread discussions about potential solutions to mitigate this recurring problem. The incident also reignited discussions about the use of alternative gloves that have been designed to reduce the likelihood of eye pokes, raising questions about why the UFC had not yet adopted these gloves despite the growing calls for change.

Central to the controversy over eye pokes in the UFC is the design of the official UFC gloves. The standard UFC gloves are constructed in a way that leaves the fighters' fingers extended forward, potentially increasing the risk of unintentional eye pokes during fights. Critics argue that this design flaw has led to numerous incidents of eye pokes and poses a significant safety risk for fighters.

In contrast, alternative gloves with a curved knuckle design have been developed with the aim of keeping fighters' fingers tucked down, reducing the chances of eye pokes. These gloves have been used in other combat sports and have been praised for their potential to enhance fighter safety. Despite the availability of these alternative gloves, the UFC has not yet adopted them, leading to growing frustration and calls for change from the MMA community.

Pressure on the UFC to Implement New Fighter Gloves

The severe eye poke incident at UFC Fight Night: Edwards vs. Muhammad intensified the pressure on the UFC to take action and implement new fighter gloves. Fighters, trainers, and commentators alike called on the organization to prioritize fighter safety and explore the use of alternative gloves with curved knuckles.

The mounting pressure on the UFC to address the issue of eye pokes also brought into focus the responsibility of MMA organizations to continuously improve safety protocols for their athletes. As the premier organization in the sport, the UFC's decisions have the potential to influence the entire MMA community, making the adoption of new fighter gloves a crucial step in enhancing fighter safety across the board.

Despite the calls for change, the UFC's response to the controversy over eye pokes has been met with complexities. While the safety of fighters is of utmost importance, the organization also faces the challenge of balancing tradition, brand consistency, and fighter comfort. The standard UFC gloves have been a longstanding symbol of the sport, and any change to their design could have ripple effects on the perception of the UFC brand.

Additionally, fighters' preferences and comfort in using the familiar standard gloves must also be taken into account. The adoption of new gloves may require a period of adjustment for fighters, potentially impacting their performance in the Octagon. Striking the right balance between fighter safety and maintaining the integrity of the sport presents a delicate challenge for the UFC.

Efforts to Address the Issue

In response to the growing concerns over eye pokes, the UFC has shown some willingness to explore potential solutions. In the aftermath of the incident at UFC Fight Night: Edwards vs. Muhammad, the UFC engaged in discussions with fighters and industry experts to evaluate the feasibility of implementing new fighter gloves.

Efforts to address the issue have also included collaboration with glove manufacturers to explore innovations that enhance fighter safety. The UFC's commitment to evaluating potential solutions demonstrates a recognition of the importance of prioritizing fighter well-being and finding effective ways to reduce the risk of eye pokes.

The controversies surrounding eye pokes in the UFC did not end with UFC Fight Night: Edwards vs. Muhammad. The topic gained further traction during the planning and execution of UFC 249. As the UFC faced challenges in finding a suitable location for the event amidst the COVID-19 pandemic, the focus on fighter safety and potential risks of eye pokes remained a central concern.

UFC 249 eventually took place with enhanced safety measures, but the controversies surrounding eye pokes continued to reverberate in the MMA community. As the UFC continues to evolve, the issue of eye pokes remains a pivotal aspect of the organization's commitment to fighter safety and athlete welfare.

Advancing Fighter Safety in the UFC

The controversies over eye pokes in the UFC have underscored the importance of continuously improving fighter safety measures. The incidents at UFC Fight Night: Edwards vs. Muhammad and the subsequent events served as a catalyst for ongoing discussions and efforts to enhance the design of fighter gloves.

As the UFC embraces the complexities of balancing tradition, brand image, and fighter comfort, it remains steadfast in its commitment to advancing fighter safety. Collaboration with fighters, trainers, experts, and glove manufacturers will continue to play a crucial role in shaping the future of fighter gloves in the UFC, ensuring that athletes can compete at their best while minimizing the risks of eye pokes and promoting the well-being of fighters at the heart of this exhilarating sport.

Chapter 24

The Betting Scandal in the UFC

On November 5, 2022, the world of mixed martial arts was shaken by a betting scandal that cast a dark shadow over the integrity of the sport. The controversy emerged following a fight between Darrick Minner, a student of UFC coach and avid bettor James Krause, and Shayilan Nuerdanbieke at UFC Fight Night: Rodriguez vs. Lemos. The bout sparked suspicion when unusual betting patterns were observed, prompting a call for a sports betting fraud investigation. This chapter delves into the details of the betting scandal, the events that transpired, and the subsequent actions taken by the UFC in response.

The firestorm of controversy erupted during the fight between Darrick Minner and Shayilan Nuerdanbieke. Minner, who was considered a large betting underdog, saw a drastic shift in odds just hours before the fight. Unusual betting patterns were detected, raising red flags among betting analysts and sportsbook operators. The sudden change in odds and the volume of bets placed on Minner prompted suspicion and warranted further investigation.

Adding to the intrigue was Minner's behavior during the fight. He threw a kick with an apparently injured leg, then surprisingly kicked with the same leg again after showing signs of injury. Shortly thereafter, he was finished by technical knockout. These events fueled speculation about the integrity of the fight and potential foul play, leading to calls for a thorough examination of the situation.

The UFC's Response and Collaboration with Betting Partner

Upon learning of the suspicious betting patterns and the controversy surrounding the Minner-Nuerdanbieke fight, the UFC took prompt action. The organization promptly informed its official betting partner, tasking them with conducting an investigation into the matter. The UFC made it clear that it had no suspicions of wrongdoing on the part of the fighters, coaches, or officials involved in the fight.

The collaboration with the betting partner was seen as a critical step in getting to the bottom of the controversy and ensuring a fair and transparent investigation. The UFC's commitment to maintaining the integrity of its competitions was evident, as it sought to address any potential breaches of rules or protocols related to sports betting.

Krause's Involvement and License Suspension

The spotlight turned to James Krause, the UFC coach, and bettor, as questions arose about his potential involvement in the betting scandal. As a key figure in the MMA community, Krause's actions and affiliations were closely scrutinized. On November 18, the Nevada State Athletic Commission took decisive action by suspending Krause's coaching license pending the outcome of the investigation.

The suspension sent shockwaves through the MMA community and prompted further scrutiny of Krause's coaching methods and relationships with fighters. The commission's decision underscored the seriousness of the situation and signaled its commitment to upholding the integrity of the sport.

UFC's Stance on Coaching and Training Affiliations

In the wake of the betting scandal, the UFC made a decisive move to address potential conflicts of interest. The organization announced that any fighter who chose to continue being coached by James Krause or training in his gym would be prohibited from participating in UFC events pending the outcome of the ongoing investigations.

The decision by the UFC demonstrated its determination to maintain the highest standards of fairness and transparency in the sport. By taking a firm stance on coaching and training affiliations, the UFC sought to ensure that fighters' training environments and coaching relationships would not be compromised by potential conflicts of interest.

In the aftermath of the betting scandal, the UFC made a significant change to its rules to address potential future issues. The organization introduced a set of rules that explicitly banned athletes, coaches, and their close family members from betting on UFC events. These rules aimed to eliminate any appearance of impropriety and minimize the risks of conflicts of interest or foul play.

The introduction of the new betting rules signaled the UFC's commitment to learning from the controversy and implementing measures to safeguard the integrity of the sport. By taking a proactive approach to address betting-related concerns, the UFC sought to protect the reputation of the organization and the trust of its fans.

Rebuilding Trust and Moving Forward

In the wake of the betting scandal, the UFC faced the challenge of rebuilding trust among fans, fighters, and the wider MMA community. The organization emphasized its commitment to transparency, integrity, and fair competition. As the investigation continued, the UFC maintained an open dialogue with stakeholders and provided regular updates on the progress of the inquiry.

The implementation of new betting rules and the decisive action taken in response to the controversy demonstrated the UFC's dedication to learning from past mistakes and preventing similar incidents in the future. The organization recognized the importance of maintaining the credibility of the sport and ensuring that fans could have confidence in the fairness of every competition in the Octagon.

Upholding Integrity and Fairness in the UFC

The betting scandal that rocked the UFC served as a sobering reminder of the importance of upholding integrity and fairness in the sport of MMA. The incident prompted the organization to take swift and decisive action, collaborating with its betting partner and implementing new rules to prevent future controversies.

As the investigation into the betting scandal continues, the UFC remains steadfast in its commitment to maintaining the highest standards of transparency and accountability. By addressing potential conflicts of interest and setting clear guidelines for betting, the UFC strives to protect the sport's reputation and ensure that fighters and fans can have confidence in the fairness of every competition in the Octagon. Moving forward, the organization will continue to learn, evolve, and strengthen its safeguards to uphold the integrity of MMA and preserve the spirit of competition that defines the sport.

The betting scandal that shook the UFC served as a wake-up call, prompting the organization to take swift and decisive action. By collaborating with its betting partner, suspending involved parties, and introducing new rules, the UFC demonstrated its commitment to maintaining integrity and fairness in the sport of MMA. Moving forward, the organization will continue to evolve and strengthen its safeguards, ensuring that every competition in the Octagon upholds the highest standards of transparency and accountability.

Chapter 25

The Merger of Titans: Endeavor and WWE Join Forces

Endeavor's IPO and Zuffa Acquisition

In April 29, 2021, Endeavor, a renowned sports and entertainment company, made a significant move in the business world by launching its initial public offering (IPO) and becoming a publicly traded company on the New York Stock Exchange. The decision to go public demonstrated Endeavor's confidence in its growth and expansion plans, showcasing its commitment to delivering exceptional value to its shareholders. With the proceeds from the IPO, Endeavor strategically seized the opportunity to acquire the remaining shares of Zuffa, LLC, the parent company of the Ultimate Fighting Championship (UFC). The acquisition valued Zuffa at a staggering $1.7 billion, making it a wholly-owned subsidiary of Endeavor.

This transformative acquisition not only showcased Endeavor's financial prowess but also its vision to expand its presence in the sports and entertainment landscape. By acquiring one of the most prominent and influential organizations in the combat sports industry, Endeavor further solidified its position as a major player in the global sports market. With Endeavor's vast network and resources, the UFC was set to embark on a new era of growth and innovation under the stewardship of this dynamic conglomerate.

The Visionary Merger with WWE

On April 3, 2023, the sports and entertainment world was sent into a frenzy with the unexpected and groundbreaking announcement that the Ultimate Fighting Championship would merge with the iconic professional wrestling promotion, World Wrestling Entertainment (WWE). The news of this visionary merger sent shockwaves throughout the industry, promising to redefine the combat sports landscape forever. The merger aimed to bring together the unscripted drama of UFC with the scripted theatrics and larger-than-life characters of WWE, creating an unprecedented fusion of sports and entertainment.

The newly formed entity resulting from the merger would be known as "TKO," which stood as a symbol of the combined strengths and potentials of both organizations. As Endeavor's CEO, Ari Emanuel, would oversee this new venture, it was a testament to his visionary leadership and his relentless pursuit of innovation in the sports and entertainment realm. By uniting two powerhouse brands like UFC and WWE, "TKO" sought to create a unique platform that would captivate audiences worldwide, transcending the traditional boundaries of combat sports and entertainment.

Vince McMahon's Role and "TKO" Leadership

With the announcement of the merger, the legendary chairman of WWE, Vince McMahon, emerged as a central figure in the future of "TKO." Serving as the executive chairman, McMahon brought with him decades of experience and unparalleled influence in the world of professional wrestling. His involvement added an intriguing layer of excitement and potential to the venture, as fans and stakeholders speculated on how his influence would blend with the dynamic leadership of Ari Emanuel and the passion of Dana White, the president of the UFC.

Speaking of White, the outspoken and passionate leader had played a pivotal role in the UFC's global expansion, transforming it into a worldwide phenomenon. His dedication to the sport and his unwavering commitment to the fighters had endeared him to fans and fighters alike. As White continued to retain his position within "TKO," he brought with him a wealth of experience and a strong vision for the future of the organization. With McMahon's expertise in the world of scripted entertainment and White's acumen in the realm of unscripted combat sports, "TKO" was poised to become a dynamic force in the sports and entertainment landscape.

The Valuation and Potential Impact

The valuation of UFC at an astonishing $12.1 billion was nothing short of a monumental milestone for the organization and the combat sports industry as a whole. The merger with WWE, a juggernaut in the entertainment world, signified a new chapter for both organizations and promised to be a mutually beneficial venture. As the valuation reflected the remarkable growth and success of UFC under Endeavor's leadership, it also showcased the immense potential and impact that the merger could have on the combat sports landscape.

The merger held the promise of unleashing exciting cross-promotional opportunities and dream matchups that had once been considered mere fantasies. However, with such a transformative move, there were skeptics who questioned how the unique identities of UFC and WWE would coexist harmoniously within "TKO." The merger signaled a potential shift in the landscape of both MMA and professional wrestling, igniting discussions and debates among fans and experts alike. Nonetheless, with the combined might of UFC and WWE, "TKO" was poised to attract a diverse and extensive global audience, transcending borders and demographics.

Anticipation and Uncertainty

As the sports and entertainment world eagerly awaited the birth of "TKO," the atmosphere was filled with anticipation and excitement. With Endeavor's visionary leadership and the legacies of WWE and UFC behind it, the newly formed company held the potential to revolutionize the combat sports industry. However, it was not without its uncertainties and challenges. The journey ahead was uncharted territory, but with the seasoned leadership of Endeavor and the iconic legacies of WWE and UFC, "TKO" had all the makings of a transformative force in the world of sports and entertainment.

As the merger became a reality, fans, fighters, and stakeholders eagerly anticipated the dawn of a new era in combat sports history. The future was bright, and "TKO" was poised to leave an indelible mark on the sports and entertainment landscape. The possibilities were endless, and the excitement was palpable as the world eagerly awaited the moment when "TKO" would step into the spotlight and make its grand debut. The stage was set, and the countdown had begun for the birth of a new era in combat sports. With its innovative approach and powerhouse partnerships, "TKO" was on the cusp of creating a new legacy in the world of sports and entertainment. The union of UFC and WWE, under the banner of "TKO," would undoubtedly redefine the boundaries of combat sports and captivate audiences worldwide.

As the future unfolded, the world held its breath, ready to witness the extraordinary impact of this historic merger. Fans would be treated to a spectacle unlike anything seen before, as "TKO" embarked on a journey that promised to merge the best of both worlds, delivering exhilarating moments and unforgettable memories. The excitement was infectious, and the anticipation reached a fever pitch as "TKO" prepared to make its mark as a trailblazer in the world of sports and entertainment. The stage was set for "TKO" to carve its path, and the world was invited to be a part of this exhilarating and transformative journey. As fans, fighters, and stakeholders joined hands in this new era of combat sports, the future of "TKO" was set to shine bright with endless possibilities.

The Future of the UFC: Forging Ahead into a New Era of Mixed Martial Arts

As the premier organization in mixed martial arts, the UFC has set its sights on an ambitious goal of expanding its global reach. With a rapidly growing international fanbase, the promotion recognizes the importance of reaching new markets and engaging diverse audiences from different corners of the world. Hosting events in various countries has been a significant step towards achieving this objective.

Looking ahead, the UFC plans to forge strategic partnerships with local organizations and sponsors to create unforgettable live experiences for fans worldwide. Collaborating with regional promotions enables the UFC to tap into a wealth of talent and showcase fighters from different cultures and backgrounds. By bringing the excitement and spectacle of the octagon to new territories, the UFC aims to solidify its position as a truly global sports phenomenon.

Embracing New Technologies

In an era of rapid technological advancements, the UFC is keen on harnessing the power of innovation to enhance fan engagement and fighter experiences. Augmented reality (AR) and virtual reality (VR) are expected to revolutionize how fans consume MMA content, offering immersive viewing experiences that make them feel like they are right there in the middle of the action.

The UFC is actively exploring ways to integrate AR and VR technologies into its broadcasts and digital platforms, giving fans the opportunity to experience fights from unique perspectives. From virtual cageside seats to interactive fighter interviews, the UFC envisions a future where fans can be part of the action like never before.

Additionally, advancements in sports analytics and data-driven insights will play a crucial role in fine-tuning fighter training and performance. By leveraging advanced data analytics, fighters can gain valuable insights into their opponents' strengths and weaknesses, allowing them to strategize more effectively and achieve optimal performance inside the octagon.

Elevating Production and Broadcasting

The UFC is committed to delivering top-tier production and broadcasting standards for its global audience. Embracing state-of-the-art equipment and broadcasting capabilities, the promotion seeks to provide fans with an unparalleled viewing experience. Enhanced camera angles, immersive audio, and stunning visual effects are some of the elements the UFC plans to incorporate to transport viewers into the heart of the action.

Collaborating with media partners, the UFC envisions exploring new broadcasting platforms to cater to the preferences of its diverse fan base. Whether through traditional television, online streaming, or emerging platforms, the UFC strives to ensure that fans can access and enjoy their favorite fights anytime, anywhere.

Promoting Athlete Welfare

With the sport of MMA evolving, the UFC places a strong emphasis on the well-being and welfare of its athletes. Ensuring fighter safety and long-term health remains a top priority for the promotion. The UFC continues to invest in sports science and medical research to better understand the physical demands of the sport and provide fighters with the necessary tools and resources for optimal training and recovery.

Through partnerships with leading medical institutions and experts, the UFC aims to stay at the forefront of athlete welfare, setting new standards for fighter care in combat sports. Additionally, the promotion seeks to implement measures to prevent injuries and promote overall fighter well-being, ensuring that fighters can compete at their best while enjoying a sustainable career in the sport.

Creating Stars and Building Legacies

The UFC recognizes the immense value of stars in shaping the sport's identity and attracting new fans. As the promotion looks towards the future, it remains committed to nurturing and promoting emerging talents. The UFC provides a platform for fighters to showcase their skills and personalities, allowing them to rise through the ranks and earn their place in the spotlight.

Shows like Dana White's Contender Series have been instrumental in unearthing hidden gems and providing them with opportunities to make their mark in the sport. By celebrating the achievements of its past champions, the UFC aims to inspire the next generation of fighters, showcasing the journey from unknown contenders to iconic champions.

Embracing Cross-Promotional Opportunities

In its pursuit of growth and expanding its global footprint, the UFC remains open to exploring cross-promotional opportunities with other organizations. Collaborating with regional promotions and partners allows the UFC to tap into new talent pools and create super-fights that capture the imagination of fans worldwide.

Cross-promotional events could potentially feature dream matchups and title unifications, providing fans with unparalleled spectacles that transcend organizational boundaries. Such collaborations hold the potential to elevate the sport of MMA to new heights, making it a true global phenomenon and widening the appeal of the UFC even further.

Advancing Female MMA

The UFC is fully committed to advancing female mixed martial arts, providing female fighters with equal opportunities and recognition. As women's MMA continues to gain momentum and attract a dedicated fan base, the UFC seeks to showcase the immense talent and skills of female fighters through marquee events and captivating matchups.

Moreover, the promotion aims to support initiatives that empower female fighters, ensuring they have access to training resources, equal pay, and promotional opportunities. By breaking down barriers and challenging stereotypes, the UFC envisions a future where women's MMA holds a prominent place in the sport's landscape, inspiring a new generation of fighters.

Fostering Fan Engagement and Community

Fans are the lifeblood of the sport, and fostering fan engagement is paramount to the UFC's future success. The promotion plans to build vibrant and inclusive online communities where fans can connect, share their passion for MMA, and interact with fighters and each other.

Through fan events, interactive experiences, and behind-the-scenes access, the UFC seeks to make fans feel like an integral part of the UFC family. Listening to fan feedback and preferences will be central to the promotion's efforts to continually improve the fan experience and create lasting connections with its dedicated global fan base.

The future of the UFC is defined by an unwavering commitment to growth, innovation, and athlete welfare. Embracing new technologies, expanding its global reach, and elevating production and broadcasting standards are just some of the ways the UFC plans to remain at the forefront of the sports world. With a focus on creating stars, advancing female MMA, and fostering fan engagement, the UFC is poised to continue its journey as the premier organization in mixed martial arts, inspiring audiences around the world for generations to come.

Conclusion

From Humble Beginnings to Global Glory: The Epic Saga of the UFC

The Complete History of the UFC takes us on an extraordinary and unparalleled journey through the dynamic evolution of mixed martial arts and the meteoric rise of the Ultimate Fighting Championship. From its humble beginnings as an underground spectacle to its current status as a global sports phenomenon, the UFC's story is one of determination, resilience, and boundless potential that has forever changed the landscape of combat sports.

In the early days, the UFC faced skepticism and controversy, with many doubting its legitimacy and long-term viability. However, through the vision and perseverance of its founders, the UFC persevered, implementing crucial rules and weight classes to bring structure and legitimacy to the sport. The emergence of skilled fighters like the Gracie family and their groundbreaking Brazilian Jiu-Jitsu showcased the effectiveness of different fighting styles, leaving a lasting impact on MMA that would shape its future.

Under the visionary guidance of Lorenzo and Frank Fertitta, and the tireless dedication of Dana White, the UFC entered a transformative era that saw strategic investments and ambitious global expansion. Their astute business decisions and unwavering belief in the sport catapulted the UFC into the mainstream, captivating audiences worldwide and establishing it as the premier MMA organization.

The introduction of The Ultimate Fighter reality show marked a pivotal moment in the UFC's history. This groundbreaking television series not only breathed new life into the sport but also introduced fans to a new generation of fighters with raw talent and compelling backstories. The emotionally charged drama of the show, coupled with the intense competition inside the Octagon, resonated with audiences and cemented the UFC's place in popular culture.

This era also saw the emergence of iconic fighters who transcended the sport and became global superstars. Conor McGregor's brash charisma and remarkable fighting skills captured the imagination of fans worldwide, while Ronda Rousey's trailblazing performances shattered barriers and elevated women's MMA to unprecedented heights. These transcendent figures, along with other legendary champions like Jon Jones and Anderson Silva, played an integral role in elevating the UFC to unprecedented levels of success and popularity.

As the sport continued to evolve, the UFC made strategic partnerships and bold moves to enhance its global reach. The ESPN era marked a historic broadcasting deal that brought extensive coverage of the UFC to a wider audience. The partnership with ESPN and exclusive content on ESPN+ provided fans with unprecedented access to their favorite fighters, events, and behind-the-scenes moments, deepening their connection to the sport.

Notably, the inclusion of women's MMA in the UFC was a monumental step forward, as fighters like Ronda Rousey and Amanda Nunes broke barriers and shattered stereotypes. Their remarkable achievements showcased the UFC's commitment to diversity and equality in the sport, inspiring a new generation of female athletes and creating new opportunities for women to compete at the highest level.

Looking to the future, the UFC remains at the forefront of innovation and global expansion. Strategic partnerships with companies like Endeavor and WWE offer exciting prospects for growth and further expand the sport's reach around the world. The introduction of advanced technologies promises to revolutionize the viewing experience, bringing fans even closer to the action and providing a more immersive and interactive way to engage with their favorite fighters and events.

As the world emerges into a new era, the UFC's legacy continues to shine bright, a testament to the power of passion, dedication, and a collective vision. From the early days of uncertainty to the present standing as a global sports powerhouse, the UFC's history is filled with moments of triumph, transformation, and groundbreaking achievements.

The Octagon has become an enduring symbol of human potential, where fighters step in with courage and determination to test their skills against the very best. For fans around the world, the UFC is a source of excitement, inspiration, and unforgettable moments that bring us together in celebration of athleticism and competition.

The Complete History of the UFC is a testament to the sport's remarkable journey and its unwavering commitment to pushing the boundaries of what is possible. As we reflect on the past, embrace the present, and eagerly anticipate the future, the UFC's legacy is one of endless possibilities. It continues to be a platform for athletes to chase greatness, for fans to experience the thrill of victory and the agony of defeat, and for the world to witness the boundless potential of human competition.

As the UFC continues to captivate the world, the Octagon awaits the next chapter in its storied history. With a wealth of talent, global appeal, and a passionate fan base, the future of the UFC shines brightly, promising even more incredible moments and stories yet to be written. The journey is far from over, and the best is yet to come for the Ultimate Fighting Championship.

Thank You for Embarking on This Journey

As we come to the end of "The Complete History of the UFC," I want to express our sincerest gratitude for joining us on this exhilarating ride through the world of mixed martial arts and the evolution of the Ultimate Fighting Championship. Throughout these pages, we have explored the highs and lows, triumphs and tribulations, and the unforgettable moments that have shaped the UFC into the global phenomenon it is today.

My goal in writing this book was to provide you with a comprehensive and engaging account of the UFC's remarkable history.

We delved into the early days of the sport, where it was met with skepticism, and followed its ascent as it captured the hearts of millions of fans worldwide. From legendary fighters to iconic events, from controversial moments to groundbreaking partnerships, we aimed to leave no stone unturned in showcasing the UFC's impact on combat sports and popular culture.

None of this would have been possible without the incredible athletes, coaches, and staff who have contributed to the UFC's success. To all the fighters who have stepped into the octagon, pushing their bodies and spirits to the limit, we applaud your dedication and bravery. Your passion for the sport has inspired generations of fans and future fighters.

I also extend my appreciation to the UFC's founders, Dana White, Lorenzo Fertitta, and Frank Fertitta III, for their vision, leadership, and unwavering commitment to turning the UFC into a global powerhouse. Without their tireless efforts and belief in the sport, the UFC would not have reached the heights it enjoys today.

Furthermore, I want to thank the fans. Whether you are a long-time follower of the UFC or a newcomer to the sport, your passion and enthusiasm are the lifeblood of MMA. Your support fuels the fighters' determination, and your unwavering loyalty has made the UFC what it is today – an electrifying and unforgettable spectacle.

As we close this chapter, I want to remind you that the UFC's story is far from over. With each passing year, new fighters will rise, records will be broken, and the sport will continue to captivate audiences around the world. I hope that this book has provided you with a deeper understanding and appreciation for the UFC's history and that it has sparked your curiosity to follow the sport's journey into the future.

Thank you once again for being part of this incredible journey. From the early days of the octagon to the global powerhouse it is today, the UFC has transcended boundaries and brought people from all walks of life together under one thrilling banner. I hope you carry the spirit of the UFC with you as we eagerly await the next chapter in this ever-evolving saga.

If you enjoyed this book, please consider leaving a review.

In the spirit of sportsmanship and camaraderie,

James Bren

Other Books by James Bren

The History of MMA
The History of the NFL
The History of the NHL and the Stanley Cup
The History of the UFC – Book 1
111 Weird, Fun, and Random *Facts About the UFC*
The History of the NHL
The History of Bellator
The History of the NBA
The History of Major League Baseball
The History of the UFC – Book 2
The History of Mixed Martial Arts
MMA Manuscripts: 30 Must-Reads in the World of MMA and Combat Sports
The History of NASCAR
The History of FIFA
The History of the PGA TOUR
The History of the Association of Tennis Professionals
The History of Wimbledon
The History of The National Rugby League
The History of the Indian Premier League
The History of Pride FC
The History of the ICC
The History of Major League Cricket
The History of Boxing
The History of the Summer Olympics
The History of the Winter Olympics
The History of the Masters

9 798230 558569

Printed by Libri Plureos GmbH in Hamburg, Germany